A TREASURY OF
HUSBAND AND WIFE
HUMOR

Edited by

James E. Myers

THE LINCOLN-HERNDON PRESS, INC.

818 S. Dirksen Parkway

Springfield, Illinois 62703

A Treasury of Husband and Wife Humor

Published by
      Lincoln-Herndon Press, Inc.
      818 S. Dirksen Parkway
      Springfield, Illinois 62703
      (217) 522-2732

Printed in the United States of America

LIBRARY OF CONGRESS CATALOGUING-IN-PUBLICATION DATA

      ISBN 0-942936-22-1 $10.95
      Library of Congress Catalogue Card Number 93-078240
      Second Printing

Typography by
      Spiro Affordable Graphic Services
      Springfield, Illinois

TABLE OF CONTENTS

INTRODUCTION

An entire generation was introduced to the healing power of laughter by Norman Cousins who, in 1979, in his book, *Anatomy of an Illness*, explained how, in hospital, he eased his pain and speeded his recovery by watching the Marx Brothers and other humorists on television. Now we know that there truly is healing power in humor. Just as we have always known that anger cannot survive mutually shared laughter. The ancient saying, "Laughter is the best medicine" is not an idle statement but succinctly phrases a truth.

Long-married couples, too, know that even their most bitter arguments, disagreements, can be washed away by shared laughter. And with fifty percent of American marriages ending in divorce, it must be clear to all that anything that can, even partially, reduce this catastrophic divorce figure must be sought out if our society is to remain based on the solid, lifetime duration of traditional marriages, based on American biblical values.

Is it possible that humor could help change the dismal course of contemporary marriage and replace stress, anger, vituperation and unforgiveness with their opposites? It's certainly worth careful consideration. As they say…"it couldn't hurt nothin'!"

But enough of the clinical approach! We must beware that as E.B. White said, "Humor can be dissected as a frog can but the thing dies in the process and the innards are discouraging to any but the pure scientific mind." Let us set aside the philosophical, medical and theological implications of humor and just consider it as pure fun, a delight and joy that helps make life…and marriage worth-while. Let us proceed on with this collection, secure in the knowledge bequeathed to us thousands of years ago, by biblical Job, no less, who said, "Enjoy life with the wife you love." And might we presume to add:"with humor."

On a more modern note…"Marriages rarely go bankrupt when a couple finds something that together they can laugh at as, for example, those old wedding pictures!"

Just remember, "There is no time [to save a marriage] like the pleasant."

1

WIVES
Sometimes They Win

"My dearest Polly," wrote her former fiancee, "I've been desolate ever since I broke off our engagement. Simply devastated. Won't you please consider coming back to me? You hold a place in my heart no other can fill. I need you so much. Won't you forgive me and let us make a new beginning? I...NEED...YOU!

P.S. By the way, I want to congratulate you on winning the state lottery."

There was a time when women went to a chiropractor to get rid of a pain in the neck. Now they divorce him.

Peter Sellinger purely loved Sadie Hawkins but he was just too shy to propose to her. Now he was up in years and neither he nor Sadie had ever been married. Of course, they dated about once a week but Peter was so timid he just never got around to suggesting marriage. But one New Year's day, he determined to ask her. He called on her on the phone: "Miss Hawkins?"

"Yes, this is Miss Hawkins."

"Will you marry me?

"Of course. Who's speaking?"

"They call it bigamy when a man has more than one wife. What do they call it if a woman has more than one husband?"

"Insanity."

Jim Thompson had a terrible argument with his wife when he told her he'd planned to go fishing next weekend. He told his buddy about it. "She wanted me to visit her mother that same weekend," Jim told his friend.

"So tell me, Jim. How is her mother?"

George tiptoes in every night, very late and half shot. Now she's tempted to finish the job.

He'd been out "on the town," one night, and came home dead drunk. In the morning, his wife awakened him and asked, "How do you want your eggs, George? Fried, boiled or intravenously?"

Husbandly courage: You can't tell much about a husband until you treat him like a watermelon ... thump him first!

Marriage certainly entitles a woman to the protection of a brave, strong, adventuresome husband, one who will hold the stepladder while she climbs it to get something from the top shelf, the jerk!

God made man and then said I can do better than that and made woman.

Adela Rogers St. John

On their fiftieth wedding anniversary, a Hollywood man was asked the secret of his long marriage, most unusual in that part of California. "Well, at home, I lead the roost," he said. "And my wife leads the rooster."

When you hear a man boast of running things at his home, you can be pretty sure that he means the washing machine, the lawn mower, the power saw, the electric drill...and errands.

Their marriage is a wonderful partnership. He's the silent one.

Edith Hause had a most difficult delivery. She now says that if the husband had every other child, there'd be only one in the family.

Oscar Ansell had a miserable day fishing on the lake where it was hot as blazes and rough as a cob. After going all day without a bite, he stopped at the supermarket and ordered four catfish. "Pick them out and then throw them at me, will you?" he told the fish salesman.

"Why do you want me to throw them at you?"

"Because I want to tell my wife I caught them."

"OK, but I suggest that you take the Orange Roughy."

"But why?"

"Because your wife came in and said that if you came by, I should tell you to take Orange Roughy. She prefers that for supper tonight."

Husband (the generic type): Most husbands are like a strand of barbed wire. They have their points.

Henry Abel's son, David, burst into the house, crying like everything. His Mama asked him what the problem was.

"Pop and I were fishing, and he hooked a giant fish. Really big. Then, while reeling it in, the line busted and the fish got away."

"Now come on, David," his mother said, "a big boy like you shouldn't be crying about an accident like that. You should have laughed."

"That's what I did, Mama."

Husbands are alike but each has a different face so you can tell them apart.

Ruth Simlack took some lunch to her husband who was fishing on the lake front. "Have you hooked any, dear?" she asked.

"Well," he replied, "if I catch this one that I'm trying for now, plus two more, I'll have three."

He's the stingiest husband in town. His wife told him that she'd like to see the world, so he gave her a map.

"YOU BROKE A HUNDRED? SO DID I!"

"What did your husband Al say when his line busted and that big bass got away?"
"Do you want me to leave out all the profanity?"
"If you please."
"Well, Al didn't utter one word."

The reason that so many families can't make both ends meet is because the man is too busy making one end drink.

There was an advertisement in a small town newspaper's personals column that read, "Peter K., please contact me at once and bring with you three rings -- engagement, wedding, and teething. And do I have news for you! Mary."

Intuition: A wife's ability to listen then read between the lines.

Housework: What the wife does that nobody notices until she doesn't do it.

Pat McHenry and his wife, Martha, were getting ready to leave home for a vacation. Martha started out the door, then stopped and said, "Pat, this time you check to see if the coffee pot is off, television plugs are pulled, burglar alarm on, doors locked, and I'll go out and blow the horn."

"Everybody says that Sally married Ed for his money."
"Yeah, I heard that, too. But if she did, she certainly earned it."

Elmer and Virginia had been dating for almost a year when, one evening, Virginia said, "Elmer, you look like my fourth husband." And Elmer, startled, asked,"How the heck many husbands have you had?"
"Three," she replied.

She's terribly mean to her husband. The other day, she hid his teeth and then...you won't believe this...she served him corn on the cob.

Women are accused of having no sense of humor. Maybe so. But if so, it's so that they can love their men instead of laughing at them.

"George, we've been wanting to take a trip to the desert for a long time," Tammy Suchert growled at her husband. "And when we get there, I'm going to leave you in the middle of all that sand, with a canteen of cool, clear **salt** water."

If you want to sacrifice the admiration of many men for the criticism of one, go ahead, get married.

Katherine Hepburn

Fay Chester was a busy housewife with a demanding husband, six children and a large house. The only relief she got from her chores was the twice-a-week bridge game she shared with a dozen other women. The only flaw in the bridge club relationship was that Fay loved to tell off-color stories and the girls didn't want to hear them.

To teach Fay a lesson, the other women decided that the next time she told an off-color story, they'd just get up, walk out, meet at another home but without Fay.

Sure enough, at the next meeting, Fay started, "You know, girls, there's a rumor going around that a busload of prostitutes will be leaving in the morning for that big gold find up in Alaska, and they say..." Just then, the women all stood up and started for the door. Fay was disconcerted but only for a moment, then she understood what was going on and said, "Hey! Girls! Hold on, hold on! There's plenty of time 'cause the bus doesn't leave till morning!"

That Pete Rosen is a terrible guy. He told his fiancee that nothing would be good enough for her and, you know what? After they were married, he still thought it was.

Joan and Alan have never stopped feuding, even though they've been married five years. Why, the very day they were married, at the altar when he said, "I do," she shot right back with, "Oh no you don't."

"Maybelle, are you satisfied with married life?"

"Satisfied? Well, I feel about that just like I do after a big, huge dinner...I don't want any more of it!"

"Pete, George told me that your wife came to you on her knees last night."

"She sure did. She dared me to come out from under the bed."

Advice to the new bride: You can't be treated like a doormat if you don't lie down.

One of the reasons that fifty percent of marriages end in divorce is that those guys who promised they'd die for their woman, just don't come through.

'Tis wisely written that a good husband is the light of his wife's life. But some wives are getting fed up with seeing their lights go out every night!

Jack McCallister had been turned into a women's libber by that dynamic, aggressive liberator of women...his wife. So, one evening at a party, Jack assumed the role of a male chauvinist now converted to a women's libber.

"I'm here to tell you folks that I've seen the light," Jack said. "I truly do believe that women are in every way the equal of men."

His wife interrupted: "Now you're braggin', Jack!"

"I want a husband who is decent, God-fearing, well-educated and sincere. Now I don't think that's too much to ask of a millionaire, do you?"

Husband and wife arguments are as natural as day and night. And Dave and his wife, Nancy, were having a humdinger. Dave took off his pants and threw them at Nancy, saying, "Hey, Woman, can you fill these pants up?"

"Of course not, you jerk. You know I can't."

"You're right. You can't. I wear the pants in this family."

So Nancy took off her panties and threw them at Dave, yelling, "Can you get into these panties?"

"Hell no! You know I can't!"

"And you won't either, until you change your treatment of me."

I like two kinds of men: domestic and imported.

Mae West

Tom Edwards was telling his friend that the way his wife had been acting, he thought that she wanted to get rid of him.

"What makes you think that?" his friend asked.

"Well, for one thing, for the last several months, instead of bringing me the morning paper, she brings me a road map!"

The clerk was showing a lady a most beautiful shirt and tie. "Now this," the clerk said, "is absolutely elegant. It will be perfect for a man-about-town."

"Could be," the woman replied, "but I'm looking for something for a louse-around-the-house."

Anytime you hear a man brag about how he runs every danged thing in his home, you can be sure he refers to the lawn mower, the car, errands and the baby carriage.

♥ ♥ ♥ ♥ ♥

"IT WON'T DO ANY GOOD TO OFFER ME A MINK JACKET, OR A NEW CAR, OR A MASTER CHARGE CARD...I MIGHT LISTEN TO A PACKAGE DEAL!"

Sarah and her boyfriend had a falling out. Sarah told him: "Anytime you happen to pass my house, I'd certainly appreciate it."

"I think it's perfectly wonderful the way the Browns get along. They seem to do everything together and have so much joy out of it."

"Yes, that's true. I'm sure the reason for it is that each does exactly as...**she** likes."

When asked why she sought a divorce, Harriet said, "That man of mine is of no more use than a needle without an eye."

Most wives love to brag about their husbands when talking to other women. A wonderful example of this conjugal happiness occurred when Sally Harney was discussing her husband. "He's simply wonderful," Sally said. "He doesn't drink or smoke or run after young girls or leave me alone nights to go bowling with his buddies. Nosiree, he doesn't do any of those things."

"You're so fortunate," exclaimed a newcomer to the community. "What is the secret to your marriage?"

"My husband is paralyzed."

It has been observed that God created man because he couldn't teach gorillas to mow the lawn or to clean the garage.

A man driving downtown with his wife said, "I've been reading the most interesting book, Dear, it's about transmigration of the soul. About coming to life as another type of being, as, for example, a yellow man, or a bird, or even a worm. Honey, do you think it possible that I could be reborn as a worm?"

"No, dear," she replied. "Souls never come back the same as they died."

Old maid: A critical reflection on every bachelor.

"YOO-HOO, DEAR, STILL MAD AT ME?"

Recently widowed, Sue Fleschman was telling a friend about the difficulties she now faced with lawyers, settling the estate. "It's been one difficult time after another, Emma. Sometimes I wish Tom hadn't died."

"Marie, I read that out in Iowa, a woman with nine kids married a man with seven. Isn't that something?"

"Sure is," Marie responded. "That wasn't a marriage...it was a merger!"

♥ ♥ ♥ ♥ ♥

"I can't believe it...you say you never quarrel with your wife?"

"That's right. When we disagree on anything, she goes her way and I go hers."

"Do you play any kind of musical instrument?" his friend asked.
"You bet. Second fiddle at home."

A man can possess guns, knives, explosives to get what he wants, but a woman has her weapons on her.

The women's club was having a lecture on Iran, and the lecturer was telling them of the greatly different relationships between men and women in Iran. "I've seen cases of a woman hitched to and working along side a donkey," the lecturer said.

One of the ladies in the audience stood and said, "That's not so strange, Mr. Speaker. We see it often over here, too."

"Tell me, Ralph," his friend asked, "how are you and the missus getting along?"

"Real fine, George," was the reply. "We just never have any arguments. In the morning, she does what she wants, and in the afternoon, well, you see, hmmm, I do what she wants."

She makes him a good and gentle wife: She hits him only with the soft end of the mop.

"Wouldn't it simply kill you if your husband were to run off with another woman?"

"Well, it might," was the calm reply. "They say that irrepressible joy can bring on a heart attack."

"Dear, something was in my mind, just then, and now it's gone before I could tell you of it."

"Well, Dear, perhaps it was lonely."

Bachelor: A fellow who has avoided the opportunity to make some woman miserable.

"God had a good purpose in mind when He made women both beautiful and dumb."

"How do you figure that?"

"Well, He made us beautiful to attract husbands and He made us dumb so we could love them."

"Elmer, you worry too darned much," his wife told him. "Worry is kind of like a rocking chair...it gives you something to do, but it gets you nowhere."

"I don't understand why you feed every tramp who comes to your home looking for a handout. And you never even ask them to work for you! How come?"

"Well, it is just so very satisfying to feed a man a meal and not have him find fault with my cooking."

VISIONARY -- Marrying a man to reform him.

Two women were talking about the husband of one. "Is he still so goldarn lazy?" Sally asked Mary.

"Sally, he's the laziest man in town, by far. It numbs his soul to have to get out of bed to eat his meals and positively shrivels his soul to have to quit eating to go back to bed."

Sylvia and Theresa were shopping when Sylvia volunteered that her husband was a completely faithful man. "He never so much as looks at another woman," she said.

"It's the same with my Harold," Theresa said. "He's too good, too decent, too kind and...too old."

The first time you buy a house, you see how pretty the paint is and buy it. The second time, you look to see if the basement has termites. It's the same with husbands!

Lupe Valez

The "good friend" hastened to tell the middle-aged matron the awful news: her husband was chasing around after a young babe in her twenties.

The matron smiled, "So what?"

The friend was surprised. "It doesn't bother you that he's running around with that chick! How's that?"

The matron said, "I have a little dog who chases cars, too."

Fred Jenkins was worried about the decline in the quality of his marriage. He made an appointment with a marriage counselor to discuss his problem.

"Do you still kiss your wife when you get home from work, show her all the little attentions you did during the first few years of your marriage?"

"No-o, I guess not," Fred replied.

"That happens with many married folks," the counselor replied. "Now I want to suggest you begin to do all those nice little things, attentions that you did the first few years of your marriage...fuss over her, buy her flowers, take candy home to her, try to be a lover instead of a mere husband."

"That sounds good to me. You're right. I'll start this evening."

When Fred got home that night, he presented his wife with several packages. He gave her a big hug and kiss and said, "We're going out on the town tonight, Honey Bun, just the two of us and we're going to have a great old time, just like the first year we were married. I got a table at the Hilton, two seats for a great musical and that's only the beginning."

His wife stared at him, then burst into tears. "What's wrong, Honey? Tell me, what's the matter?" Fred cried.

"Well, Susie came home from high school today and told me she's pregnant. Then the grocer called and said we'd used all our credit and he needed the money tomorrow or we'd find ourselves in court. Jerry is in the hospital with an attack of appendicitis. I busted the fender backing out of the garage and now...now" she broke off and sobbed.

"Now what, Honey, tell me, tell me," Fred begged.

"And now you come home drunk."

"How do you like that lovely glass vase on the mantle?" Mrs. Spikre asked her friend, "they hold the ashes of my late husband."

"I didn't know your husband was deceased," her friend replied.

"He isn't. But that's where he puts his cigarette ashes and if he doesn't stop it, he's sure as hell gonna be!"

When Tom and Peggy celebrated their fortieth wedding anniversary, Tom asked, "Remember the promise we made to each other when we got married, Peggy?"

"You bet I do," she replied. "We promised to be faithful to each other, didn't we?"

"Yep! Sure did. And we promised that if we ever were unfaithful to one another, we'd put a kernel of corn in a jar and then, on our fortieth wedding anniversary, we'd compare notes, or I should say, kernels."

Tom got his jar and dumped the kernels on the table. There were fifteen kernels and he flushed and stammered an apology to Peggy.

"Don't feel bad, Tom," Peggy reassured him. "To be unfaithful to me only fifteen times in forty years is a real compliment to me."

"Well, where's your jar, Peggy?" Tom asked.

"I'll get it now," she said and walked to the cupboard and dumped nine kernels of corn onto the table. "I'm proud of you, Peggy," Tom said. "But I notice a five-dollar bill in the jar and some change. What's that for?"

"Well," Peggy said, "When the price of corn went way up, I sold a bushel."

"ORVILLE IS SO USED TO CHEATING – LAST YEAR WHEN HE MADE A HOLE IN ONE, HE WROTE DOWN ZERO!"

Arnold and Isabelle Hankins had been married twenty-five years when they agreed to a divorce. After the divorce was granted, that same day, they celebrated with a special dinner. After the soup, Arnold asked if Isabelle would mind him asking an intimate question. "Not at all. Go right ahead," she replied.

"Well, there is one thing that has always bothered me. We have five kids with black hair but the youngest, Jimmy, has blonde hair. Whose kid is Jimmy?"

"I just can't tell you, Arnold. I'm afraid it would hurt you too much."

"I'll be fine. Now that we're divorced, how could it hurt me?"

"Well, if it's that important to you, I'll tell you. Jimmy is your child."

A man should never question his wife's judgment. Look whom she married!

Margaret Summers had gone to visit her mother in another city and she had left her husband to fend for himself. She left him a list of items he would need to complete the foodstuffs required while she was gone. The list read:
1.   Chicken
2.   Cucumbers
3.   Green peppers
4.   Sweet rolls
5.   Canned vegetable soup
6.   Bread
Mr. Summers went to the market and came home with one chicken, two cucumbers, three green peppers, four sweet rolls, five cans of soup and six loaves of bread. Seems that he ate very well in her absence.

Mary Simpson advised her brother, now in love: "Don't tell your lovely one that you are unworthy of her...just let it come as a surprise."

Vivacious 42-year-old divorcee seeks new husband with similar personality. Must have own teeth.

Some people will do anything to lose weight. Consider the case of Marietta Brown. She was having coffee with a friend and said, "I'm fed up with my husband. He's so mean to me, he makes me jittery and that makes me lose weight."

"Well, why don't you dump the beast!" her friend said.

"I plan to do that, but first I want to get down to 110 pounds."

"You seem to like the many ways he pays attention to you...so why don't you marry him?"

"Because I like the many ways he pays attention to me."

Fed up with her husband's constant grousing, his wife shouted, "You promised that if I married you, you'd be humble and grateful."

"Well, that's just what I am!"

"Wrong. You're grumbly and hateful."

Marie Peters is a very good wife. Why, just let her husband get home late at night and as soon as he enters the door, he gets his pipe, slippers, PJs, robe, book and, if anything else is handy, she heaves that at him, too.

Husband: "You seem preoccupied, Dear. What's bothering you?"

Wife: "I can't help thinking of the time when one of us will have to go and leave the other alone and lonely."

Husband: "Don't worry about it, Sweetheart. Get it off your mind."

Wife: "I can't help worrying about it. Still, when it does happen, I think I'll move to Florida."

The male is a domestic animal who, if treated with firmness and kindness, can be trained to do most things.

Jilly Cooper

"They tell me your husband loves to read...reads all the time. Why, he must be a bookworm."

"No, not really. He's just the ordinary kind."

Marriage counselor to female client: "Maybe your problem is that you've been waking up grumpy in the morning."

Client: "No, I always let him sleep."

Compromise -- an amiable arrangement between a man and his wife whereby they agree to let her have her own way.

Mary Simpson was thirty-four years old and her mother despaired of her ever finding a husband. Then, one evening, Mary brought home a lovely, if rather stupid-looking young man whom she introduced to her mother. Then they had dinner. It started to rain hard and there was thunder and lightening so that Mary's mother said to the visitor, "It is far too wet out there for you to go home tonight. Now you just sit there and Mary and I will fix up our spare room so you can stay here tonight, OK?"

The young man agreed to stay the night. Mother and Mary went upstairs to ready the guest room.

When they got back downstairs, the visitor was standing there soaking wet and dripping water all over the floor.

"Where...what...how come you're so wet?"

"I had to go home to get my pajamas."

Mary Jo Swanson was suing her husband Joe for divorce. Her lawyer asked, "Mrs. Swanson, do you think your husband is of sound mind?"

"I don't quite know how to answer that," Mary Jo replied.

"Well, in your judgment, is he crazy?"

"I...I...I really can't say."

"From the way you say that, we can assume you think him crazy?"

Mary Jo thought a bit about that, then gave this spongy reply: "Y'know, I don't think I'd call him crazy. Let me say this, though. If he was loose, why, I doubt that they'd lock him up. On the other hand, if he was locked up, I don't think they'd dare set him free."

Susan Jenkins has come upon a rule she considers true as gospel, i.e., in carrying things from the kitchen to the dining room, the less you have, the more you spill.

♥ ♥ ♥ ♥ ♥

A man came to the door of the Estill home, rang the bell and Mrs. Estill answered the call. "Good afternoon, Ma'am. I'm looking for Mr. Estill."

"I'm Mrs. Estill. What can we do for you?"

"Nothing, thanks. It has to do with our Fishing Club. Could you tell me where to find Mr. Estill?"

"Sure. Just go to the big pond back of our house and look for a stick with a worm on both ends."

Dave Carpenter

"Of course I'm not always right. I married you!"

Here's a good remedy for a husband's excessive boozing when he's away on a fishing trip.

Pete Smith's wife, Karen, was fed up with all the beer consumed by her husband during his weekend fishing jaunts. So she hit on this method of curing him.

When Pete had been off fishing this particular weekend and had opened his lunch box to get something to eat, he selected a lovely sandwich, bit into it only to find it filled with beer bottle tops!

Give a man a free hand and he'll run it all over you.

Mae West

"Oh, Mrs. Brown," cried her neighbor, "I'm so sorry to hear about the loss of your husband. He was such a wonderful man. I'm sure he left you well provided for, didn't he?"

Mrs. Brown dabbed at her eyes and muttered, "Yes, he was such a wonderful husband, and he left me a hundred thousand dollars. I miss him so much that I'd give fifty thousand to have him back!"

"Did you hear about Suzie's husband...who drowned in a huge vat of beer?"

"Oh, how horrible."

"Yes, but it wasn't all bad for him. He got out twice for pretzels!"

A man thinks he knows, but a woman knows better.

"Emma Stokes fired her husband's beautiful new secretary before the month was up."

"But why? He hardly gave her a chance."

"It wasn't her. She didn't want to give **him** a chance."

No wonder Loren Funk can't get a job. He's just too lazy to get out and hunt one. Why last week at the local department store, there was a power failure and Loren was trapped for thirty minutes on the escalator.

19

When asked to define the difference between lovers and husbands, Maizie Doaks replied, "Day and night."

"The doctor told me I needed more exercise," the husband told his wife.

"That's obvious," his wife replied. "So what are you doing about it?"

"Well, as you know, I used to watch golf on T.V.," he replied. "But from now on, I watch tennis."

Marcella Vespa called her friend Winona about the disappearance of her husband, who had been missing for several days. When asked by the police for a description of her husband, she replied: "He's over six feet tall, with beautiful, wavy blond hair. He's got a fetching smile that shows a perfect set of teeth. He wears Brooks Brothers clothes and is muscular, weighing about two hundred pounds."

Winona waited until Marcella had finished her phone call, then asked what it was all about. "Your husband is a tad over five feet and his hair is gray and almost gone. He grins like a polar bear and he's bought every darned tooth in his head. Marcella, that was an untrue description of your husband."

"Sure it was," Marcella replied. "But who wants that jerk back?"

"It's kind of like breaking the umbilical cord, this business of having your son graduate from college. I don't know any other way to describe it," she said to hubby.

"Perhaps a more appropriate description or word would be 'purse strings,'" hubby suggested.

"George, I'm sorry about that flat tire," his wife said. "Would you mind if I came out to the garage with you and listened to you fix it?"

"Wow, that peacherina looks like a million!" Florin Barton said as he ogled the cute young thing crossing the sidewalk.

"I don't think so," his wife gritted back. "She's a few years short of that -- but you're close."

Josephine was an avid fisher but her husband wasn't. She bought a fishing rod for him and displayed it at the Women's Fishing Club monthly meeting, telling the girls, "This is the best rod I could buy. I got it for my husband."

One of the women said, "What a deal. I'd sure like to work a swap like that for my old man."

The next meeting of the Women's Fishing Club was held at Mary Toskin's home. All the fisherwomen gathered in front of the fireplace to admire a huge shark that was stuffed and hung over the mantle. "I caught that beauty," she explained to the women, "while fishing in the ocean with my husband. I'm so proud of it and I hope you can do the same."

"It's a beauty," one of the ladies remarked. "But what's it stuffed with?"

"My husband."

Hubby: "Wow! I just banged my crazy bone."
Wife: "Put your hat on and nobody will see it!"

Emmett Piersen was a fussy fellow. He yelled at his wife, "What do I have to do to get a glass of water in this house!"

"Try setting yourself on fire," his wife coolly replied.

A guy was very rude to his wife when she offered him sugar for his coffee. He yelled, "What's the matter with you? You ought to know I hate sugar. I never use it in my coffee!"

His wife quietly said, "Why? Because it's refined?"

Mary Tompkins, daughter of farmer Eric Sands, was always trying to teach her father correct English. So when Eric mentioned that he was going to spend the day spreading "manure" on next year's cornfield, his daughter said, "Daddy, please watch your language. I wish you'd say fertilizer instead of that horrible word 'manure.'"

But her mother said, "Don't be impatient, dear. It took me three years to get him to say 'manure.'"

♥ ♥ ♥ ♥ ♥

First old maid: "I heard that Maizie Donner just had her fourth husband cremated."

Second old maid: "Wouldn't y'a know! I can't get even **one** husband, yet others have 'em to burn."

♥ ♥ ♥ ♥ ♥

There was a guy in Keokuk, Iowa who was so cheap that when his doctor recommended that he and his wife take a trip to the mountains for her health, the tight jerk bought her a five dollar picture of the Rocky Mountains and fanned her with it.

"OF COURSE I'D STILL LIKE YOU IF YOU WERE BROKE, I'D MISS YOU TOO."

"Never go to bed angry. Stay up and fight."

Phyllis Diller

Eddie George was the laziest man in Virden, IL. They say that he was dead for five days before his wife noticed. He's the guy that claimed not to be at all lazy and that he'd work any and every week...that didn't have a Thursday in it.

Husband: One who stands by his wife in troubles she'd never have had if she hadn't married him.

The alcoholic's wife:	"My husband has caught a terrible cold!"
Her friend:	"What's he doing for it...starving it or feeding it?"
Wife:	"Neither. He's flooding it."

"If men are God's gift to women, then God must really love gag gifts."

A popular senator, well into his seventies, surprised everyone by marrying his secretary who was some thirty-five years younger. They went on an extensive honeymoon and were greeted by the press on their return to Washington.

As he stepped off the plane a reporter asked, "Tell us, senator, how was your honeymoon? Enjoy nice weather?"

The oldster sighed. "The weather was fine but the humility was awful!"

♥ ♥ ♥ ♥ ♥

There was a woman in New Berlin, Illinois, who got rid of 185 pounds of flabby fat in a mere 90 days. She divorced him.

And it's still a good joke, the one about the two old friends who met on the street. "I hear you're going to get married again," one girl said.

"Yep! I'm marrying an undertaker. That makes number four for me."

"I remember your husbands real well. The first was a banker, the second an actor and the third...let's see now...oh, yes, he was a minister. And now your fourth husband is an undertaker. Any special reason for your selections?"

"You bet there is. It's one for the money, two for the show, three to get ready and four to go."

If you think a woman can't take a joke, just take a look at the men some of them marry.

Elmer Rankin's family lived in the hills of Kentucky and their oldest son, Joshua, was approaching puberty. As often happens, Joshua had begun to act most peculiar, moping about until one day his Mamma asked, "Joshua, what on airth is the mattuh with ya?"

Joshua replied that he was needing a girl but that everyone of the girls he liked--the pretty ones, cute and curvaceous--were cousins according to his father. "I asked him about Sara Jane, then Cindy Sue, and I even asked him about Mandy. He said I shouldn't touch any of 'em, that they was all kin to him."

Joshua's mother put down her broom and turned to Joshua. "Oh, is that all," she sighed. "Now Joshua, you just go on and do what your heart...or whatever...tells ya to do 'cause your daddy ain't no kin to you."

Good advice from a mother to her marriageable daughter: "Dear, I advise you never to trust a husband too far or a bachelor too near."

"A man with two wives is called a bigamist. Just what do they call a man with three wives?"

"A pigamist."

"What's new?"

Reprinted with permission of the **Saturday Evening Post**

When Elmer Rankin came home from the audiology department of St. John's Hospital, he was sporting a brand new hearing aid. His wife was surprised and pleased to see it. "Oh, I'm so glad you finally got your hearing aid," she said. "You certainly needed one. I hope you bought a good one."

"Oh, I did," Elmer assured her. "It's the best you can get."

"Great. I bet it cost plenty."

"Oh, it did. Seven hundred smackeroos. It wasn't a cheap one, no, sir."

"Seven hundred dollars? For a hearing aid? Wow! What kind is it?"

Elmer looked down at his watch. "Quarter to six," he replied.

Men are those creatures with two legs and eight hands.
Jayne Mansfield

Honesty is frequently the best policy between husband and wife. Consider the husband who asked if his wife would remarry, should he suddenly die. "Yes, I suppose so," she said.

"And would you stay in this same house with your new husband?"

"Oh, I suppose so."

"And would you allow him to wear my clothes?"

"Probably."

"And my golf clubs? Would you give them to him?"

"That I wouldn't do," she replied emphatically, "he's left-handed."

Of course, it is true that women sometimes make fools of men. But most guys are the do-it-yourself type.

It's not the men in my life that count -- it's the life in my men.
Mae West

Old George has been around a long time and has seen many things change. Recently, he observed that women have finally succeeded in coming down to the humiliating position of almost absolute equality with men.

It is true that most men run the show at home. But it is also true that their wives write the script.

"I tell you true!" the preacher announced from the pulpit, "There has been only one perfect person in all of history -- Jesus Christ. Do any of you good people know of another?"

There was a pause and then an elderly lady stood.

"I take it, Sister, that you have known a second absolutely perfect person?"

"Not myself, Pastor. But I sure have heard a great many things about this second perfect and wonderful person. Seems she was my hubby's first wife."

There's a bumper sticker going the rounds that reads, "I still miss my husband, but my aim is getting lots better."

Polly Meiers was sick and tired of her husband laying around the house all day, rarely looking for a job, providing the home with almost nothing to eat or sleep on. One day, she'd had enough and called to her husband to come to the kitchen. "It's the mayor on the phone," she told him, "and he wants to tell you that you've been nominated for the GOYA CLUB."

"What the devil is that?" her husband asked.

"It stands for...GET...OFF...YOUR...ASS. Get it?"

"Susie, I heard today that Emily is really sorry she divorced me. Not that I'm sorry because now I have you. But isn't it amazing that she would say she's sorry she divorced me?"

"Freddie, like I've always said...wives are just like fishermen...they complain about the one they caught and brag about the one they let get away."

Mary Keyes had certain and definite opinions about most everything and she didn't hesitate to tell her husband what they were. One day, hubby Paul said, "Mary, only fools are certain. The wise person hesitates."

"Are you certain about that?" Mary asked.

"Yes, Mary, I'm sure, absolutely, positively, undeniably certain of it."

A tough old boy born and raised deep in the heart of Texas got sick and died. Since he was well known in his town, the funeral was well attended. The minister delivered a stunningly laudatory sermon, saying how good a father the deceased had been, how charitable he was, how much everybody in town thought of him and how generous he had been to the church. It was one of the most complimentary sermons ever heard in those parts.

The widow was seated in the front row, surrounded by her several children. She leaned over to the one next to her and said, "Slip up there, dear, and make sure it's really your paw in that casket."

"Mary, I heard that you lost your husband last year."

"Yes, it was a terrible shock for me."

"Well, you look just fine, now. I hope he left you well-fixed. I can see that you have a new ring. It's a beauty. It must be at least ten carats, right?"

"Yes, a bit more than that. But I'm very proud of it."

"I take it he left you quite a bit of money? Am I right?"

"Well, he did leave me ten thousand dollars and suggested that I get a large stone in his memory. This is the stone."

"WHAT EVER HAPPENED, RUTH? YOU USED TO BE A FUN PERSON!"

When you see what some girls marry, you realize how they must hate to work for a living.

Helen Rowland

A man in the house is worth two in the street.

Mae West

At last, one for Mama. It seems that the bride was beside herself with all the details needing attention for the wedding. "Everything has got to be just right, Mama. We must take care of every insignificant detail."

"Not to worry, Dear," Mother said. "I'm sure he'll show up."

Bryan Reilly came out of the doctor's office looking kind of concerned. "The doctor said I had to lose weight...or else," he told his wife as they walked out of the doctor's office.

"It's amazing, Bryan," she said. "I was just thinking, when you told me how much weight you'd put on, that a white oak tree with a circumference the same as yours would be sixty-eight feet tall."

In all systems of theology, the devil figures as a male person.

Don Herold

You know women's lib has gone a bit far when you hear someone say, "Women the lifeboats!"

"My wife divorced me for reasons of health," Pete Robbins sadly told his friend.

"Gosh, I thought you were in excellent health, Pete," his friend replied.

"You don't understand," Pete said. "She got sick of me."

My husband and I never agree on anything, except for one thing; he doesn't think anything is too good for me and neither do I.

It was reported in VARIETY that Milton Berle, while watching television, asked his wife, "Do you feel that sex and excitement have gone out of our marriage?" And his wife, Ruth, replied, "I'll discuss it with you during the next commercial."

"Doggone it, Paul, I asked you yesterday, again this morning and now, for the third time, when...are...you...going...to quit procrastinating?"
Paul glanced at his persevering wife over the morning paper. "Honestly, we'll just have to wait and see."

"I can't marry you, Eddie," Mary Lou told her boyfriend. "You are a salesman. I prefer a man who builds things, who makes things, like an engineer who...makes half-a-million dollars a year."

"I've been married for thirty years. My wife and I have an agreement. She takes care of the little things and I take care of the large things."
"Wonderful! Could you tell me how it works?"
"Not really, because to date, no large things have come up."

Attorney: "I don't understand how you can risk it again, Mrs. Hall. You've had three husbands and they've either gone insane or turned out worthless. Why would you want to take such a risk for yet another?"
Client: "I want...well, you see...I just want a safe and sane **fourth.**"

When the work-happy plumber died,
   His wife with humor grim,
Decided, (she knew his habits well),
   To bury his tools with him.

Poor provider husband: When he enters to apply for a job, it's the same as three good men leavin'.

"Paul and I have been married for two years and we have yet to quarrel. If we have a difference of any kind, and I am right, Paul nods and accepts my opinion."

"But what if he's right?"

"That hasn't happened."

Barney Roven was truly a hen-pecked husband. He and his wife were walking downtown when they passed a scale. "I think I'll weigh myself," Barney said, and he did. When the card with his weight on it was thrust out, he took it, read his weight, then turned the card over and read his fortune, "You are strong, energetic, sexy, courageous and a good provider."

Said his wife, reading the card over his shoulder, "And they didn't get your weight right, either."

Freedom, in the marital state, has been defined as the liberty that allows a man to do exactly that which his wife pleases.

Because of the shameful number of divorces occurring every year, it has been recommended that we name the divorce action, "Deciduous Divorce." You get rid of him in the spring and marry another in the fall!

Elmer Fisher called the office and told the boss he'd be unable to work for a few days, saying, "My wife broke an arm."

"Sorry to hear that, Elmer, but why does that stop you from coming to work?"

"Well, y'see, um-m..er...well, it was my arm she broke."

There was once a woman whose improvident husband died while shopping. It seems that the dumpster lid fell on him.

WIDOWHOOD -- The only compensation some women get out of marriage.

The doorbell rang and Mrs. Jones went to the door. It was the repairman from the utilities company. "We got a call from you, Mrs. Jones, and I'm here to repair whatever it is you said was not working. Could you tell me where it is?"

"Sure can. He's upstairs in bed."

Said a fair-headed maiden of Tarmack,
"Of you, I'm exceedingly fond, Jack.
　　To prove I adore ya,
　　I'll dye, darling for ya
And be a brunette, not a blonde, Jack!"

After a bitter argument with his wife, Tom Nottings said, "Well, I can tell you this...a woman is nothing but a rag, a bone and a hank of hair!"

His wife shot back: "And man is nothing but a brag, a groan and a tank of air!"

The question was asked, "Why do women pay so much more attention to their appearance than to improving their minds?" Patricia Altgeld responded: "Because, while most men are stupid, few are blind."

A customer entered the Waldenbooks bookstore and asked the first clerk he met, "Do you have a book with the title *Man, The Master of Women?*"

"Certainly, Sir. You'll find it in our fiction department."

Knock, knock.
　　Who's there?
Effervescent.
　　Effervescent who?
Effervescent for wine, women and song, he'd be a perfect husband.

A widow is one who now can find no fault with her husband.

"Were you ever married, Johnny?" his girlfriend asked.

"Yeah, I sure was. But the dingbat ran away while I was taking a bath."

"Boy, I'll bet she waited years for that opportunity."

Elmer Stoopenfumble was a cheap guy who constantly scolded his wife for her extravagance. Anything she bought seemed to cost too much.

One day at the table, she remarked, "I wonder what women angels wear in heaven?"

"I know what you'll wear," her husband replied. "The most expensive stuff they got up there."

"Now don't you worry, Elmer," his wife said. "You won't be there to pay the bills."

New neighbors had moved in next door and Mrs. Edwards was much interested in them. After a few days, she reported to her husband: "Stan, they seem a much-in-love couple. Each time he leaves the house, he kisses her. Now, Stan, why don't you do that?"

"Good Lord, Emma," Stan said, "why I hardly know her."

A wife is a companion who sits up with you whenever you are sick and, somehow, manages to put up with you when you are not.

"You ask if I really and truly know my own husband? Why, Agnes, I can read him like a book."

"Good. Just be sure you stick with your own library!"

♥ ♥ ♥ ♥ ♥

I miss my husband so,
    The woman cried.
And so just one more shot
    At him she tried.

There is absolutely no excuse for a wife to have an inferiority complex. All she has to do to avoid or correct it, is to be sick in bed for a day, leaving her husband to manage the household and the kids.

♥ ♥ ♥ ♥ ♥

HE AND SHE
When I am gone, you'll find it hard,
      Said he.
To ever find another man like me.

What makes you think, and I suppose
      You do,
I'd ever want another man like you?
                  Eugene Fitch Ware

♥ ♥ ♥ ♥ ♥

A man is king on his own throne, that is, until his wife overthrows the monarchy.

You may think you've seen lazy men. Well, let me tell you, you haven't seen the half of it until you consider Zeke Buffer. Why, he's so lazy that one time he handed his wife five buttons and said, "Here, Mabel, sew a shirt on 'em, will ya?"

Elsa Szold had a new neighbor with whom she became quite friendly. In a discussion over coffee, the neighbor told Elsa how much she admired her husband's piety. "I watch him every morning when he gets in your car to drive to the office," the neighbor said. "He's so pious and starts his day with a blessing."

"Thank you so much," Elsa said to her neighbor, "but you got it all wrong. What my husband does, when he gets in the car, is not a blessing, but a check to see that he's got his glasses, his cigarettes, **and** that he's zipped."

Danny Sullivan was a model husband and neighbor. He not only helped his wife in all things around the house, but helped other people, too. For example, he noticed a lady edging her car this way and that in a tiny parking space. Danny stood in front and directed her until she was parked securely in the tiny space. "Thanks a million, Sir," the woman said. "But I was trying to get out."

Every mother generally hopes that her daughter will snag a better husband than she managed to do...but she's certain that her boy will never get as great a wife as his father did.

Joy and Seth Thomas had a dozen guests for dinner and after eating, they were all assembled in the living room, talking, having a relaxed time of it when Joy and Seth's little girl burst into the room, her clothes dripping wet. She was so upset that the poor little thing could hardly get her words out. "You...you...nut!" she said, pointing to one of the male guests. "You left the seat up!"

Susie Jenkins is real careful about food. She serves only food that is low in calories and high in trading stamps.

Gossip columnist: "My dear, your husband looks entirely different tonight. It must be that new suit he's wearing."

Movie star: "Nope. New husband."

Income Tax Examiner: "Mrs. Fredericks, what's your husband's average income?"

Mrs. Fredericks: "Oh, about midnight."

The young woman left her husband and returned home to her mother where she explained that the marriage was done, finished, kaput. Her husband simply drank continually.

"But if you knew he drank that much, why did you marry him?" her mother asked.

"Well, Mama, I didn't know that he drank...until one time he came home sober!"

The puny little guy walked into the bar and joined a crowd of huge men lined up at the bar. He had a drink and then told the big guys that his wife had told him to come home after just one drink.

Of course, the big guys all sneered and said, "What are you, man or mouse?"

"Heck fire, guys, I'm a man," the little guy said.

"What in hell makes you so derned sure of that?"

"Well, I'll tell you," the little guy said. "My wife is scared of mice."

♥ ♥ ♥ ♥ ♥

Sylvia Etter tells why she loves to garden and is so good at it. "I put on a wide-brimmed hat," she said, "and a short but loose-fitting dress. I hold a small towel in my right hand and a martini in my left. Then I'm ready to tell my husband where to go to begin digging, harrowing, planting and weeding."

♥ ♥ ♥ ♥ ♥

Worthless husband: His mama should have stayed a virgin.

Sarah Levy never married although she was beautiful and charming. When asked why, she explained, "I have a dog that growls and snarls a lot, a fireplace that smokes, a parrot that cusses like crazy and a physician who looks me over regularly. So tell me, why do I need a husband?"

Susan Pickering, a housewife, answered the door to find a man who was soliciting money for a poor woman just down the street. "She owes for groceries, electricity and she's several months behind in her rent," the man said. "Could you help out with a contribution?"

"It's mighty nice of you to take on such a thankless task," Susan told him. "Of course, I'll help. But tell me, Sir, just who are you?"

"I'm the landlord!"

Most mothers don't care much about taking their excess weight off, they just wish they could rearrange it.

The guy really loved his whiskey. But one night, on the way home, he stumbled and fell on his bottle, cutting himself badly. And so, as soon as he got home, he got a box of band aids and began to apply them over all the cuts.

The next morning, his wife was furious and he wondered how she knew he'd been drunk the night before.

"How'd I know?" she screamed. "You plastered band aids all over the full-length mirror in the bathroom."

"I don't understand you women," Josh said to his wife. "You go to a movie and cry like crazy over troubles of folks you don't even know and who don't even exist. How do you explain it?"

"Well," his wife replied, "it's about like the way you guys howl and cheer and yell yourselves half hoarse when a ball player you never met hits a home run when other men -- whom you don't know either -- are on all three bases."

George Tobias ran for office and was defeated. But he took that defeat like a man...he blamed it on his wife.

"One of the things that has puzzled me all of my married life," said the harried housewife, "is how this man of mine can manage to look like he's cleaned the entire house after dumping only a simple ashtray."

"Every time I need some money, I have a heavy argument with my husband," Susie Poppins told her friend. "I almost always end by telling him I'm going home to mama, if he doesn't come across."

"How effective is that?"

"Works every time. He gives me money for the plane ticket."

Earl Hodges was nearing 60 years of age but he was wonderfully active, jogging and playing racquetball and tennis. His wife asked a friend if her husband was still active.

"You bet he is," the friend replied, grinning. "Each week he's out seven nights running."

A husband is a guy who:

   He tells you when you've got on too much lipstick, and helps you with your girdle when your hips stick.

   Ogden Nash, "Marriage Lines," Little Brown & Co.,1949

Larry Reynolds had a drinking problem, and his wife was fed up with him. So, on this one night when he came blundering into the house, he wound up in the bathroom where he stumbled about and found himself in the shower, turned on the water by accident, then yelled for the missus to come help him. She came in the bathroom, sized up the situation as he got more and more drenched, call him all kinds of a so-and-so, and told him where he was heading.

"You're right, dear," the drunken guy admitted. "But let me in, will you, it's raining powerful hard out here."

Sharon Tasbort was a nut about golf. And she played almost every day. Finally her husband got fed up with her daily absence and said, "If you spent just one complete day with me instead of on that damned golf course, I think I'd fall dead."

"Look here, Honey," she replied, "there's no use your trying to bribe me!"

Two women were talking in the supermarket. "I'm furious with my husband Tom," one of them said. "He took up fishing this spring, and since then he's gone every weekend and often during the week. I'm really mad! Why he seems like a complete stranger."

"Aren't you lucky!" the other woman said.

Mary Simpkins was a wise mother. When her daughter had matured sufficiently to be aware of marriage, she advised her thusly: "Dear, there are two ways to get yourself a husband and you should know what those two are. First of all, a girl should exhibit a generous nature. That's most important! But if that is not feasible, then she should show how generous nature has been to her."

If a mother wants a bit of time to herself at the end of the day, she can find it one place only...doing the supper dishes.

A woman who is wise has the good judgment to make her husband feel as if he truly is the head of the house when, as a matter of fact, he heads only the entertainment committee.

Some guys are just too darned meek for this world. Consider the bookkeeper who had been suspicious of his wife's fidelity for a long time. So he decided to see for himself. He left work to go home where, sure enough, he found a hat and an umbrella on the table and his wife on the couch with another guy. Furious, the meek guy grabbed the umbrella and broke it across his knee and said: "There! Now I hope it rains."

They'd gone to a community dance because it was their tenth anniversary. On the dance floor, he whispered in her ear, "My sweetest, dearest wife, life was a desert before I married you."

"That," she replied, "probably explains why you dance like a camel!"

" OH, GOOD. THERE'S MY OTHER KNITTING NEEDLE ! "

| Woman to her beautician: | "When you get done with me, will my husband think I'm still beautiful?" |
| Beautician: | "I sure hope so, Ma'am. Does he drink a lot?" |

"Harry thinks he can sing, and he does try to do it every chance he gets."

"That's great. So Harry is a singer."

"No, I didn't say that! He **thinks** he can sing. Actually, he even laughs out of key. So I bought him a trumpet."

"A trumpet? For a singer? Why?"

"Because when he plays the trumpet, he can't sing."

In Arkansas, they tell the story about a farmer who was so lazy that when he got the Seven Year Itch, he ended up eleven months behind in his scratching. And that was in spite of his wife's help at scratching!

| Country wife: | "Got to hang up now, Mabel. I'm taking my husband and his mother to the hog auction." |
| Mabel: | "How much do you think they'll bring?" |

Did you hear about the woman who told the judge she wanted a divorce because her husband was careless about his appearance? "Do you mean he is slovenly and disgusting in dress?" "No," the woman replied, "not that. What I mean is the jerk hasn't made an appearance in more than a year."

"Tomorrow is hubby Jim's birthday," Edith told the women gathered for a bridge party. "Great," one of the women said, "what are you getting for him?"

"Make an offer," Edith replied.

41

"Ted, I got a report from our mutual friend, Susan Todd, that you were at the fairgrounds and that you'd been drinking again."

"Come on, now. How could she tell?"

"She said you got off the roller coaster dizzy and staggering and you were vomiting. Then you said to her, 'I kinda think I took the wrong b-b--bus.'"

♥ ♥ ♥ ♥ ♥

Bob Thomas was nearing eighty years of age, in good health, trim and vigorous. And he was disgustingly proud of his physical condition. One day at lunch, he was bragging to a lady friend: "Would you believe that these very teeth are all my own?" he said.

"Good to hear," the bored lady remarked. "When did you finish paying for them?"

♥ ♥ ♥ ♥ ♥

"Eddie, please stop bringing up those old issues, ancient problems we had long, long ago. There's no use in our burying the hatchet if you're going to erect a marker on the site!"

Mother and Father were having a hard time getting their little boy Jesse to go to Sunday School. "I'll go," he said reluctantly, "but I bet Pa never had to go when he was a kid my age."

"Yes, he did, Jesse," his mother assured him. "He most certainly did go every Sunday."

"OK, I'll go. But I bet it won't do me any more good than it did him."

Sunny LeGlaire's ex-husband passed her on the street one day and she knew he wasn't doing well just by the looks of him. "Are you still on relief, Peter, and are they giving you the necessities of life?"

"They are," Peter responded, "but half the time it isn't fit to drink."

When Harry read the news of the marriage of the lovely Hollywood star to an unattractive, undistinguished fellow, he remarked to his wife, "Isn't it amazing how the biggest jerks manage to marry such lovely, attractive women?"

"Well, thank you, dear," his wife said, "that's the nicest compliment I've had in many years!"

She was a mighty pretty thing as she trudged from the elevator to the doctor's office. When called to enter and state her troubles, she said, "Doctor, I'm bothered by a miserable wart and I'd appreciate having it removed. Can you get rid of the wart for me?"

"I'm a doctor," the physician replied. "The divorce lawyer is four doors down the hall."

"George," Mary Hahn said, "Don't do that again. When you sneeze you should always hold your hand over your mouth."

"But why?" George asked.

"To catch your teeth."

Then there was the overbearing wife who shouted at her husband, "Quit that constant beating around the bush. If you have anything at all to say -- shut up!"

♥ ♥ ♥ ♥ ♥

Judging from the high rate of divorce, one would think that most women have not yet decided on whether to have a hubby or a hobby.

When Elliot Jason died, his wife decided to have his remains cremated. Accordingly, the undertaker presented her with several varieties of boxes and vases in which she could place Elliot's ashes. But she rejected them all. "I plan," she said, "to put his ashes in an hour glass on the mantle. That way, the lazy bum will finally be working a steady job."

Husband: "Dear, we've been home an awful lot lately. What do you say we go out on the town and have a good time tonight?"

Wife: "Hey, that's a swell idea. But if you get home first, don't forget to leave a light on for me."

♥ ♥ ♥ ♥ ♥

Wife: "Dear! Take a look at those soldiers gawking at that lovely young girl passing by."

Husband: "Soldiers? What soldiers?"

" MY HUSBAND IS LOSING HIS MEMORY, BUT I CAN'T COMPLAIN - - I'VE HAD THREE BIRTHDAYS THIS YEAR. "

At the breakfast table, Eddie Jones was reading the newspaper. Suddenly he grunted, then said, "It's sure amazing how such insufferable jerks manage to get the most wonderful wives."

"Why, thank you ever so much," his wife responded.

♥ ♥ ♥ ♥ ♥

"Dr. Jonas, please help us and do something for my husband. He snores something terrible from the moment he falls asleep until he awakens. He sounds like a freight train!"

"He may need something serious like an operation, and we hate to do that," responded the doctor. "Does it really trouble you all that much?"

"Trouble me? Doctor, it discombobulates the whole congregation."

♥ ♥ ♥ ♥ ♥

"Tell me, Susie...how did you manage to break your husband's habit of staying out till all hours of the night?"

"Well, one night when he came home late, I called out, 'Is that you, Harry?' Y'see, my husband's name is George."

♥ ♥ ♥ ♥ ♥

Mary Parr left her husband, saying that he was just too close with a buck, so tight that he squeaked when he reached for his wallet. She said he resembled a Scotchman with his natural sense of generosity removed!

♥ ♥ ♥ ♥ ♥

It was a quadruple marriage, four men who were best of friends, had just married four girls who were also very good friends. After the ceremony, they met at the hotel dining room and, while the men went outside to smoke, the excited brides talked. They soon got around to discussing their thoughts on the forthcoming nuptial night and agreed that they'd compare notes the next morning. Since they couldn't discuss matters before their husbands, they agreed on the code word, "morning." That word would describe how many times they'd made love.

At breakfast, the first two brides began to talk. "Good morning, Mary," one said.

"Good morning to you and isn't it a lovely morning?"

The third bride remarked, "It's a great morning, all right, as nice a morning as I've recently seen since the morning of the last fourth of July."

The fourth bride looked around, then said, "What a rotten day!"

Definition of a bachelor: A nice enough fellow except that he has cheated some nice girl out of her alimony.

Hubby: "Seems to me like all the weight you put on, Dear, is below your waist."
Wifey: "Yep! And it seems like all the weight you put on, my chickadee, is between the ears."

Edna Forsyte had tried to convince her husband that he should reduce, had tried for over a year, but her efforts had failed. Finally, when her husband arrived home in a brand new green polo shirt with white horizontal stripes, and the neighborhood kids began playing football on him, he was convinced!

"WAIT A SEC ... DID YOU SAY FORSAKING ALL OTHERS?"

The elderly couple sold their home and moved into an apartment. When asked by a friend how they liked their new style of living, the old fellow replied, "I like it a lot. From the bedroom window, I can watch the sun rise."

His wife replied, "Me, too. Why, he lets me watch the kitchen sink."

Liza Peters was worried about her husband. He'd been very sick yet did appear to be recovering. But now she couldn't awaken him. She frantically called the doctor. "Doctor Howard, my George has been sleeping for hours and I can't seem to awaken him. What should I do?"

The Doctor began making suggestions when suddenly Liza interrupted him. "Never mind, Doctor. I think he's OK, he just tried to blow the foam off his medicine."

Edgar Jones stood still listening to his wife try to start the car. She seemed unable to get the job done, so Edgar yelled to her through the back door, "Hey, Emily, did you try choking it?"

Emily's reply was, "No, not yet. But I sure as heck feel like doing it."

Nasty husband: There ain't a thing wrong with that feller that a good cremation wouldn't cure.

One day a salesman stopped by the Tom Jenkins farm, knocked, and Tom's wife, Mabel, came to the door. "Is your husband home, Ma'am?" he asked.

"Sure is. He's over to the cow barn."

"Well, I got something to show him, Ma'am. Will I have any difficulty finding him?"

"Shouldn't have. He's the one with the beard and mustache."

Homely husband: He's so derned ugly the flies all stay on the other side of his pickup.

The young bride asked her mother, "Is it true that the way to a man's heart is through his stomach?"
"Depends," the mother replied.
"Depends on what?"
"On what he's hungry for."

It is altogether fitting and proper that a collection of husband and wife anecdotes should begin with a poem celebrating the first pair known to mankind...Adam 'n Eve, who lived in a State of Euphoria, known as Eden.

ODE TO EVE

O Mother Eve, I do believe that after all you're glad you ate
That fruity prize that made you wise as any college graduate;
I think you thought (I'm sure you ought) the taste that made you win a sense
Of what you are, is better far than vegetative innocence!

O Mother Eve, I do not grieve though to our primal Pop you lent
That fatal bite that put a blight on Eden's treasures opulent;
Though cold and wide, the world outside was big with possibilities,
While for a wife the Sheltered Life is packed with puerilities.

O Mother Eve, you gained reprieve from commonplace transparency,
Although you trod on thorny sod, and sailed on many a barren sea;
Yet you might fly from spots too dry, or move from spots too saturate --
No Paradise so newly nice as any furnished flat you rate!

O Mother Eve, you now deceive our eyes with dress and drapery;
Around your waist are garments laced to make it small and tapery.
(If I had time to write the rhyme, I think I could contrive a list
Of gains unsought your apple brought, to stagger a revivalist!)

Edwin Meade Robinson -- 1875-1945

There was a young lady in Pascuglia,
Who said to her man, "What a pigua."
    He answered, "My dear,
    Is it manners you fear?
Or do you refer to my figua?"

Her favorite nickname for him is "Hon." As in, Atilla the "Hon."

Here's the way Joanie Tapon put down her hubby the other day. Paul, her husband, called to say that he'd be working late that night. She simply breathed into the phone: "Honey, can I count on that?"

He took his defeat just like a man ought to do...he blamed it on his wife.

Ellen Tobias was fed up with her husband, Tom. The guy couldn't hold a job, chased all the women he had energy for and was never home. So she packed up and walked out the door, only to turn and say, "Tom, I hope to run into you some other time...when I'm driving and you're walking!"

Be very, very careful about the man who claims to be boss at home. He probably lies about other things, too.

Woman's chief asset: The imagination of the male.

A good husband is one who thinks almost as much of his wife as he does of himself.

♥ ♥ ♥ ♥ ♥

Worthless husband: He ain't worth the oxygen he uses up.

Large family: They got so many kids they done wore out four storks.

Even larger family: Them folks got enough kids to bait a trot line.

Susan Evers had just suffered the loss of her first boyfriend. But her mother consoled her by saying: "Don't worry, Susie. Men are like buses. If you miss one, another will be along in a few minutes."

"I'LL NEVER FORGIVE YOU FOR THE DREAM I HAD. YOU AND BURT REYNOLDS FOUGHT OVER ME AND YOU WON!"

There is a town in Italy where the law requires a guy who gets a girl pregnant out of wedlock, to pay a set sum of money every month for fifteen years, as child support. Adhering to this rule, a certain fellow had faithfully made payments for twelve years and the mother had been sending the child to collect the money every month.

One month, the girl arrived for the check and the father told her to tell her mother that this check was the last he was giving her and that she should notice the expression on her mother's face.

The girl did just that but was back in an hour to tell her father, "I told Mama that this was the last check you were sending and that you told me to watch the expression on her face. She told me to tell you that if this truly is the last payment, then I should tell you that you aren't my father...and that I should watch the express on **your** face!"

He's got a real drinking problem. His wife Mary calls him her Optician because he's always making a **spectacle** out of himself.

"The boss said he hated to do it," Stan Guralchik related, "but the firm had to cut expenses and he had to do his duty as he saw it. So he cut my salary."

"His duty as he **saw** it, eh," Stan's wife said. "Well that man needs glasses!"

Woman's work that's never done is, more than likely, what she asked her husband to do.

"But I am tolerant of you," Jack Myers said to his wife. "It's just that I disagree with you."

"OK, then," she replied. "You certainly have a right to your ridiculous opinion."

♥ ♥ ♥ ♥ ♥

God gave women a delicious sense of humor...so they could better understand the jokes they married.

A wise man was once asked why God acted like a thief, stealing a rib from Adam while he was asleep. The wise man replied, "If someone gave you secretly an ounce of silver and you returned publicly twelve ounces, would you call that stealing?"

♥ ♥ ♥ ♥ ♥

Why is a man more easily pacified than a woman? Because man was made out of soft earth and woman out of hard rib.

♥ ♥ ♥ ♥ ♥

Oscar Levant to Harpo Marx upon meeting Harpo's fiancee: "Harpo, she's a lovely person. She deserves a good husband. Marry her before she finds one."

♥ ♥ ♥ ♥ ♥

Many men who claim they are not at all interested in marriage, have wives at home to prove it.

BEULAH'S BABIES

Miss Beulah Jones...once turned up at Columbia Hospital, a Washington institution that specializes in maternity cases. Although at Columbia for the usual reasons, Beulah made a point of insisting that she was unmarried.

"That's a bit unusual," said the clerk who interviewed her. "What's the father's name?"

"Smith -- Leonard Smith," Miss Jones replied.

She was admitted, and her baby was born in due course, no further questions asked. And in about a year she was back again.

"Well, Beulah," said the same clerk, "back again. I suppose you're married now."

"No, not yet," said Beulah.

"Who's the father this time?"

"Leonard Smith."

Another year went by, and the same thing happened again.

"Why in the world don't you marry him?" the clerk asked this time.

"Well," said Beulah, "he just doesn't appeal to me."

While she was waiting for the members of her monthly bridge club to arrive, Edna Brown happened to pass a large amount of gas. To hide the odor, she grabbed a can of air freshener and hastily sprayed the room.

And not a moment too soon, because the first guest arrived a few minutes later, sniffed, then remarked, "Good Lord, Edna! This room smells like somebody dumped on a pine tree!"

What differentiates men from government bonds?
Generally, bonds mature!

Why are jokes about women so short?
So men can remember and tell them.

What do men and whiskey bottles have in common?
They're both without content from the neck up.

You ask why Sally buried her husband George twelve feet under? Well, it was because deep, deep down, he was a good guy.

Jack told his wife, Helen, that he wanted to spend his vacation where he'd never been before. Helen said, "How about the kitchen?"

How many men does it require to change a roll of toilet paper? Nobody knows. It has never happened.

"Anna, what do you consider to be a man's idea of a seven course dinner?"
"Well, that's an easy one...a pizza and a six-pack."

DAVE CARPENTER...

"Oh, wait a minute. He must be up. The sun just went behind a cloud."

"Helen, what in the world do you do with all that grocery money I give you?"

"You'll get a good idea if you'll just stand sideways and look in the mirror!"

Mabel says there are only two things wrong with her husband...everything he says and everything he does.

"You ought to think more highly of me, Joan," her husband said. "Husbands like me don't grow on trees, y'know."

"I know...they swing from them."

He's so wishy-washy that you can't get him to take a stand on anything. His wife calls him Contraceptive because he's always avoiding the issue.

She finally got a divorce from Frank. She even called him Druggist because he was such an awful pill.

Marrying a man is like buying something you've been admiring for a long time in a shop window. You may love it when you get it home, but it doesn't always go with everything in the house.

Jean Kerr

I'd marry again if I found a man who had 15 million and would sign over half of it to me before the marriage and guarantee he'd be dead within a year.

Bette Davis

Someone once asked me why women don't gamble as much as men do and I gave the commonsensical reply that we don't have as much money. That was a true but incomplete answer. In fact, women's total instinct for gambling is satisfied by marriage.

Gloria Steinem

There's almost nothing my husband wouldn't do for me...at least, he's done nothing so far.

Can you tell me the difference between a man and childbirth?
Sure! One is terribly painful and almost unbearable while the other is just having a baby.

What has eight arms and an IQ of 80?
Four guys watching a game of football.

Why do men get married?
Because their mothers won't put up with their lazy nonsense any longer.

A man's home may seem like his castle on the outside; inside, it's more often his nursery.

Jonathan Evans was nearly one hundred pounds overweight. His wife said she'd like him better if she could see less of him.

Joe Spoon is really cheap. Why, he once told his wife to go to the dress shop and pick up some quality things...but not to get caught at it. And once, when she wanted a fur coat, he gave her a gun and a trap.

Some husband are mighty thoughtful. One such is our neighbor. He always leaves the lawn mower where his wife can find it easily.

Some married women regret that, at the wedding, they didn't keep the bouquet and throw the groom away.

The wise wife understands that the best way to keep a husband is...in doubt.

Plenty of women married men while thinking they'd be real comforters -- only to discover they were merely wet blankets.

Many an idealistic woman considers marriage as a union of two souls only to find herself hitched to a heel.

Wives seem to agree that one distinct advantage a man has is that he doesn't have to kiss someone who has not shaved for two days.

Elmer Winters always said: "The smart guy keeps both feet on the ground." "But," his wife said, "that's incomplete. He must also wipe them before coming in the house."

Don't criticize your wife before you stop to consider that the very defects you find in her may have kept her from finding a better husband than the one she got.

Sally Thomas asked why men act like morons.
Barbara replied, "Who says they're acting?"

Teddy Baer isn't very neat or clean. The other day, they weighed the dirt he cleaned from his nails! It weighed twenty pounds!

There is one rule for which there are no exceptions: If it has tires or testicles, it'll be lots of trouble.

"The best way to get husbands to do something, is to suggest that perhaps they are too old to do it."

Shirley MacLain

Mary Simkin's mother never got along well with her daughter's husband, Ted. But Ted almost kicked her out of the house when the old lady told him, "It's just too damned bad, Ted, that your mother kept you instead of the stork that brought you."

But Ted just about got even with her when they were deciding on guests for a party they were giving. "I think your mother should come, Mary. There's always room for one bore at every party."

When his mother-in-law arrived for the party, Ted couldn't resist saying to her: "You give me a royal pain in the neck!"

To which he got this reply: "Ted, you give me a pain, too, but it is about two feet lower!"

On their 25th wedding anniversary, he said, "We've been through so much, my dear, so very, very much together...and most if it was your fault."

Elmer Schlagel was away from home on business in another city. When he called home, his wife told him, "Elmer, they had your name in the obits today."

"What! In the obituary column! That's not only disgraceful but bad journalism. I'll sue 'em."

"Tell me, Elmer," his wife asked tremulously, "wh...wh...where are you calling from?"

A wife whose name doesn't matter,
　　Saw she was getting fatter and fatter.
So she dieted too well and now looks like hell,
　　And her hubby has no place to patter.

Marriage: Not a word, but a sentence (more or less).

Did you ever hear of a glow-worm marriage? That happens when the man gets the glow and the woman gets the worm.

♥ ♥ ♥ ♥ ♥

Mary and Tom Fuller were at breakfast, each reading the morning newspaper. Tom was into a section concerning life expectancy, and was amazed at one statistic. "Mary, do you realize," he said, "that every time I breathe, someone dies? Isn't that awful?"

"That's mighty interesting, Honey," Mary said, nodding. "Why don't you try mouthwash?"

♥ ♥ ♥ ♥ ♥

Man: Something like a tack that is useful only when it has a useful head...and is pointed in the right direction, will withstand repeated blows without bending. Even then such a being can go only so far as the head is willing.

♥ ♥ ♥ ♥ ♥

Mrs.: The title of a job with heavy duties, light earnings and no recognition.

♥ ♥ ♥ ♥ ♥

"In the course of the last forty years of my life, I have held many jobs. I have been a cook, window-cleaner, upholsterer, concrete-mixer, home-decorator, carpenter, electrician, typist-secretary, bookkeeper, parking attendant, shoe shine girl, plumber's helper, kennel attendant, housemaid -- to name a few -- and all for one boss...my husband."

♥ ♥ ♥ ♥ ♥

Standing at the gate to heaven, Albert noticed arrows pointing to two paths. One was marked "WOMEN" and the other, "MEN." He took the path assigned to men and followed to come upon two more gates. The right-hand gate had a sign that read: MEN WHO WERE DOMINATED BY THEIR SPOUSES. The other gate read: MEN WHO WERE BOSS AND DOMINATED THEIR SPOUSES. The first gate had an endless line of guys waiting, but only one little guy stood before the male-domination gate. Albert was undecided, so he walked up to the little guy standing all alone and asked, "Why are you standing here, a little punk like you?"

The little fellow replied, "I haven't a clue. My wife told me to stand here."

♥ ♥ ♥ ♥ ♥

If I were a girl I'd despair; the supply of good women far exceeds that of the men who deserve them.

Robert Graves

2

HUSBANDS
Sometimes They Win

"Dear, I'm puzzled," Old Joe Smith said to his wife. "Every time I figure a way to make ends meet, somebody or something moves the ends."

☆ ☆ ☆ ☆ ☆

"Of course, you should go on a diet, Dear," Mary Swanson said to her husband.

"I don't know why," he replied. "I don't eat more than I ever did."

"That's where you're wrong. More and more, you exceed the feed limit."

☆ ☆ ☆ ☆ ☆

He calls his wife Brown Sugar because she's sweet and refined!

☆ ☆ ☆ ☆ ☆

"You know, Dear," Fred Wavell said to his wife, "I'd be happy to follow the good advice 'pay as we go' if we could only finish paying for where we've been."

☆ ☆ ☆ ☆ ☆

"I don't tell my kids what my Dad told me, 'that a penny saved is a penny earned.'"

"Why not?"

"Because a penny earned and saved today isn't worth fooling with!"

☆ ☆ ☆ ☆ ☆

Her husband, Jim, was terribly nasty. In fact, they called him Bus Driver because he was always telling her and everybody else where to get off.

"George, doesn't it give you a headache, sitting all day and fishing off our boat dock?"

"No, dear, quite the opposite end."

☆ ☆ ☆ ☆ ☆

Steve Stone, at age 65, had noticed his sex drive was beginning to wane more than somewhat! So he checked in with his doctor who told him to exercise and that the preferred form of sport was jogging. Steve left the office with instructions to call back in a week. He started jogging that evening. As per instructions, he called back in a week and the doctor asked how he felt. "Great," Steve replied. Then the doctor asked, "How's your sex life?"

"Heck fire, Doc, I don't know. I'm a hundred miles from home!"

☆ ☆ ☆ ☆ ☆

Near Herford, Iowa, there is a rather sizable factory that hires only married men. Concerned about this, a local woman called on the manager and asked him, "Why is it you limit your employees to married men? Is it because you think us women are weak, dumb, cantankerous...or what?"

"Not at all, Ma'am," the manager replied. "It is because our employees are used to obeying orders, are accustomed to being shoved around, know how to keep their mouths shut and don't pout when I yell at them."

☆ ☆ ☆ ☆ ☆

Talk about diplomats! Elder Jenkins is the best. He never forgets his wife's birthday. But he always forgets which one it is.

☆ ☆ ☆ ☆ ☆

A fisherman dropped into his favorite bar. He was holding a brand new fishing rod. "By gosh, that's sure an elegant rod you got there."

"Yep! It's a good one. I got it for my wife."

"What luck! I wish I could work a deal like that."

☆ ☆ ☆ ☆ ☆

"I know you don't like my mother much, Theresa, but I hope you'll get to like her after she lives with us for awhile."

"Well, I'm trying."

"Yes, very!"

"Martha! You've been at my vodka again."

Peter Elder had a reputation for stretching the truth when it came to fishing. So he bought a scale and took it with him to his favorite hole. He'd insist on weighing every fish he caught, just to prove that he didn't exaggerate.

After several months of buoying his reputation with that scale, he announced that his wife had just had a baby and that the doctor had borrowed the scale to weigh the baby.

"And how much did the baby weigh?" his friend asked.

"I don't rightly understand it," Peter Elder said, "but the doctor weighed him the same day he was born, and he weighed over thirty-two pounds."

☆ ☆ ☆ ☆ ☆

She married a fellow named Pfeister
Weith triplets, the Lord one day bleicester.
   He looked at that trio
   And shrieked, "Oh my gawd oh!
Derned fool, whatever posseicester."

"My wife is a history buff," Tom told his friend. "She's constantly raking up the past."

☆ ☆ ☆ ☆ ☆

Before he married her, he swore that he'd do anything for her...even go to hell for her. She's made him keep his promise.

☆ ☆ ☆ ☆ ☆

Bill Kessler confessed to his wife that he really was getting bald. "It seems that my hair has gone through three stages," he said, "parted, unparted, and now, departed."

☆ ☆ ☆ ☆ ☆

"I got some good news to report," Mary Townsend told her husband. "That new freezer we ordered is coming tomorrow."
"I didn't know your mother was coming for a visit."

☆ ☆ ☆ ☆ ☆

He was a confirmed atheist before he got married, simply could not be made to believe in hell. But now that he's married, he knows that he was wrong.

☆ ☆ ☆ ☆ ☆

How does George meet a matrimonial crisis? With a firm hand...full of gifts and flowers.

☆ ☆ ☆ ☆ ☆

"Hey, Sweetheart, here's a job perfectly suited for your mother. I think you should have her apply for it."
"I'll bet you're going to suggest something real nasty for her."
"Nope. It says here the U.S. Army is advertising for someone to go to Serbia."
"What are they supposed to do there?"
"Teach the Serb military how to fight as dirty!"

☆ ☆ ☆ ☆ ☆

The first and only time she said "yes" to him was the day he proposed.

Sarah and Dick Myers were having dinner with a couple they'd not seen for several years. Each couple tried to recapture knowledge of the other by recounting their histories. "And soon after we were married," Sarah began, "we were blessed with a marvelous, chubby creature with cute bow legs and no teeth."

"You had a baby, I presume," said the other husband.

"Nope," Dick broke in, "Sarah's mother came to live with us."

Men should never marry a woman for her beauty alone. That is rather like buying a house because you like the way it's painted.

"I think you should quit gambling, dear. It's getting you no place."

"You know how it is...I win one day and lose the next."

"You do? That gives me an idea. Why don't you gamble every other day?"

"How do you like my new haircut, dear? Now I don't look like an old man, do I?"

"Nope. You look like an old woman."

An early saying has it that, "the penalty for getting the woman you want is that you must keep her" (or so it used to be).

Lionel Strachey

Zeke Tobias had lived all of his life on a farm in Arkansas, far removed from town and modern conveniences. When he was fifty years old, he and his wife Becky took their first trip to Little Rock. They visited a department store and stood in front of the first escalator they had ever seen, trying to figure what made it go up and down. They watched a little old lady take the escalator up and then disappear only to be replaced on the downward stairs by a lovely, curvaceous blond. Zeke watched the blond undulate her way as the moving stairs carried her down. Then he said to Becky: " That's some business they got going up there. Amazing! Becky, why don't you take that moving stairs on up and go through that business up there! Then we'll see what you look like when you come down."

"Zeke, did you ever marry that Arkansas hillbilly girl you were goin' with for so long?"

"Yep. Finally. Y'know her old man took a shot at me. That convinced me to marry her."

"Did he hit you?"

"Nope, but that danged bullet come so close to my head that I heard it twice."

"Twice? How come twice?"

"Once when it passed me and once when I passed it."

☆ ☆ ☆ ☆ ☆

Hunters say that marriage is the only sport where the animal captured has to buy the license.

☆ ☆ ☆ ☆ ☆

Percy Bower came home from work one night to discover that his wife had a brand new hair style. He looked at her, then said, "have you been to the beautician or are we having an electrical storm?"

"FORGIVE ME DEAR. . . I OPENED MY OWN MAIL BEFORE I THOUGHT."

He has learned to respect the saying, "A word to the wife is sufficient. Just say yes."

☆ ☆ ☆ ☆ ☆

Tom Everett was an avid reader. From the time he got home from work until he went to bed, his head was buried in a book. His nice wife, Thelma, was tired of his neglect of her.

"Tom, I'm jealous of all those books you read. Sometimes I wish I were a book. Then, I guess, you'd look at me now and then."

"Hey, Thelma, that's a great idea. If you were a book, I could take you to the library and exchange you for something a helluva lot more interesting."

☆ ☆ ☆ ☆ ☆

It is therapeutic to praise your wife. Just don't worry if the first few times it frightens her.

☆ ☆ ☆ ☆ ☆

Husband: "Holy smokes, Dear, are we gonna have corned beef and cabbage again tonight?"

Wife: "Quit griping. After all, you loved it on Monday and Tuesday and said it was swell on Wednesday and Thursday, so now, all of a sudden, you don't want it on Friday. You're mighty hard to please."

☆ ☆ ☆ ☆ ☆

Norm Jones's wife is not so very bright. The other day, she was in the supermarket when a friend rushed up to her saying, "Judy, Judy, come quick. Someone is stealing your car."

So Judy rushed outside but soon came back.

"Did you catch him?" her friend asked anxiously.

"Nope," she replied. "But I got his license number."

☆ ☆ ☆ ☆ ☆

He has suddenly discovered why God created Adam first. It was Adam's last chance to say something!

☆ ☆ ☆ ☆ ☆

A husband is a man who gives up privileges he never realized he had.

One of the oldest yet very best stories involves a woman who had triplets. "And you know that triplets only happen once in five hundred thousand times?" Mary Ellen said to her friend.

"Really!" her friend replied. "How on earth did they find time to do their housework?"

☆ ☆ ☆ ☆ ☆

Mary Simpkins bought a bottle of spot remover that her husband, by mistake, drank for booze. And now the poor guy has been missing for six months.

☆ ☆ ☆ ☆ ☆

Did you hear about the man whose wife was so hairy that he had to keep her locked in the house during the hunting season.

☆ ☆ ☆ ☆ ☆

The lady bragged too much about her clothing. "I got this handbag in Portugal and my shoes in Italy and my dress came haute couture from Paris."

"Wonderful," her neighbor replied. "But I guess you got your figure in the kitchen."

☆ ☆ ☆ ☆ ☆

Fred and Dorothy Wassell were having their usual loud and endless argument about family reunions. At last, Fred relented. "I'm awfully sorry, Sweetheart. I didn't mean all those hateful things I said about your family. As a matter of fact, I like your mother-in-law a whole lot better than I do mine."

☆ ☆ ☆ ☆ ☆

"Woman is such a contrary creature," Zeb Stork said to his buddy. "Consider the Garden of Eden. Why, they had oranges, peaches, bananas, cantaloupes, watermelons, plums, persimmons, figs, dates and lots more, and what did Eve want? An apple!"

☆ ☆ ☆ ☆ ☆

My wife's idea of roughing it is staying at a Ramada Hotel where they have only single-ply toilet paper.

"On second thought, it does taste like mother's!"

Harry and Jimmy Brown were brothers but lived different lives. Harry had a wife and a nice home while Jimmy owned and lived on a small boat, alone. Curiously, on the day that Harry's wife died, Jimmy's rowboat sank out of sight never to be refloated.

A week or so later, a nice old lady, a friend of Harry's wife, came up to Jimmy, mistaking him for his brother, Harry, and said, "I'm so sorry about your loss."

Jimmy responded, "Oh, don't bother yourself about her, Ma'am. She was kind of a useless thing from the start. Her bottom was half rotten and she smelled fishy. The very first time I rode her, she made water faster than anything I ever saw.

"Then one day, some guy used her and when he returned her, she leaked like a sieve! Four guys borrowed her last week and although I warned them what to expect, they used her so hard she cracked right down the middle... ."

Jimmy quit talking when he saw that the poor old lady had fainted.

A sweetheart is a bottle of wine, a wife is a wine bottle.

Boudelaire

☆ ☆ ☆ ☆ ☆

It was only a few days before Judy's birthday and her hubby, Stan, asked what she'd like for a gift.

Judy replied, "I really don't think I should say."

Stan: "How about a diamond and ruby ring?"

Judy: "I don't like either of them."

Stan: "Would you consider a mink coat?"

Judy: "I hate furs."

Stan: "Well, then, let me get you a golden necklace."

Judy: "I already have four."

Stan: "Please, Judy, please tell me what you want!"

Judy: "I want a divorce."

Stan: "I really wasn't planning on spending that much money."

☆ ☆ ☆ ☆ ☆

There was a young fellow named Slammer
Who had an unfortunate stammer.
    "The p-p-pain of my life,"
    Said he, "is m-my wife,
D-d-double d-d-damn 'er!"

☆ ☆ ☆ ☆ ☆

Emma Southers was explaining to her husband how much fun they'd had at the beach during her bridge club annual outing. "But," she told him, "it didn't end all that great for me."

"Why, what happened?" he asked.

"Well, I went out to take a swim in the rough water. I didn't go out so far because the waves were very bad, but even so, I suddenly noticed that all the turbulence had caused the lower half of my bathing suit to be snatched off. I looked but it was gone, gone, gone!"

"Well, for goodness sakes, Emma, what did you do?"

"Do? Why I did what any respectable housewife would do. I covered by face and eyes with my hands and ran to the beach house as fast as I could."

☆ ☆ ☆ ☆ ☆

They say that she speaks 149 words a minute with gusts up to 169.

Elmer Jokisch says that his wife is really money-hungry, that when pay day arrives, he puts his paycheck on the kitchen table...then jumps back! Elmer also accuses his wife of being a lazy housekeeper. She is so bowlegged, that she looks like a donut with a bite out of it.

But Elmer is so lazy that he rides his bike down **brick** streets to knock the ash off his cigarettes.

Here's more scuttlebutt on Elmer's fat wife. Why, Elmer has to grease the bathtub so she can get in. Her one redeeming feature has been her love of animals. Accordingly, she is the size of an elephant, laughs like a hyena, talks like a parrot, kicks like a mule, walks like a penguin and strongly resembles a hook-nosed hawk.

Her two beloved dogs up and died one day. She so loved them that she took them to the taxidermist, who asked, "Do you want them mounted?" She replied, "No, just have them look lovingly at each other."

One time, Mrs. Jokisch stepped on one of those newfangled, Speak-Your-Own-Weight machines. It said, "One at a time, please."

☆ ☆ ☆ ☆ ☆

Mr. and Mrs. Jens Swensen were known as the ideal couple with hardly a dispute, harsh word, nasty remark between them. Jens explained it this way: "We get along great because every morning, she does what she wants. In the afternoon, I do what I...ahemm...I do what she wants."

☆ ☆ ☆ ☆ ☆

Sid Edwards was discussing wives with his pal, Eddie Snow. "Sid," Eddie asked, "is your wife talkative? Mine sure is. How about yours?"

"Talkative?" Sid replied. "Well, let me put it this way. Last month I had a bad cold for three days. I lost my voice. And my wife never knew it!"

☆ ☆ ☆ ☆ ☆

Sara George was talking to the doctor about her tenth pregnancy. The doctor was upset with her, saying, "Mrs. George, I told you that you should have no more babies. You almost died with the last one. Now here you are again."

"Well, I know I shouldn't be, Doctor. But I can assure you that it won't happen again. I have a new hearing aid and it's wonderful."

"What on earth does a hearing aid have to do with you getting pregnant?"

"Well, before I got it, every night when George would say to me, 'Shall we go to sleep or what?' I'd always say, 'WHAT?'"

71

By all means marry; if you get a good wife, you'll be happy. If you get a bad one, you'll become a philosopher.

Socrates

There's this woman who plays cards one night a month with a group of her friends. And every time she awakens her husband because it's after midnight when she gets in. So one night she decided she won't disturb him. She gets home after midnight and undresses in the living room, and with her handbag over her arm, she tiptoes nude into the bedroom -- only to find her husband sitting up in bed reading.

He looks up from the paper at her and says, "Good Lord, did you lose everything?"

☆ ☆ ☆ ☆ ☆

John is very religious but the one thing that worries him is reincarnation. He's afraid that if he comes back as a dog, his wife is certain to return as a flea.

"Look on the bright side, Glenda. You weighed 110 pounds when we were married, which makes you the only investment of mine that has doubled."

The husband was in court and was catching hell from his wife's lawyer. "I think you are the most despicable man I know," the wife's lawyer shouted. "I cannot think of a more despicable, disgraceful act than your deserting your wife!"

The husband looked the lawyer straight in the eye and said, "Sir, I am not a deserter. I am a refugee."

☆ ☆ ☆ ☆ ☆

There are a few old coots around who can recall when their wives put food into a can rather than taking it out.

☆ ☆ ☆ ☆ ☆

Recently there was an announcement in the scientific world stating that, since the invention of the girdle, women are taking up one-fourth less space in the world.

☆ ☆ ☆ ☆ ☆

Johnny Pierce was looking over the gals at a party where most were clad in a minimum-of-cloth dresses. All he could say was "Low and Behold!"

☆ ☆ ☆ ☆ ☆

The following story contains a lesson for every married man. It seems that the President of a major corporation had obtained a new and very beautiful secretary. Although married and the father of four kids, the executive fell madly in love and finally accepted her invitation to dinner in honor of his birthday. When he arrived at her apartment, she told him that they would have a drink elsewhere, then return to her apartment for dinner and an "interesting" evening.

Things went swimmingly. They returned to her apartment and she excused herself, saying, "I'll be in my bedroom, honey, changing into something more comfortable, and you come on in, in five minutes." When the five minutes ended, he removed his clothes, knocked on the door, and entered, only to be met by the office force singing, "HAPPY BIRTHDAY TO YOU!"

☆ ☆ ☆ ☆ ☆

George Burton says that when he has an argument with his wife, words fail him.

A husband and wife are in bed and the wife snuggles up to hubby and says, "Sweetheart, how many others were there before me?"

After a few minutes, the wife says, "Well, I'm waiting."

And the guy takes a deep breath and says, "Well, I'm still counting!"

☆ ☆ ☆ ☆ ☆

A beautiful blonde in a convertible pulls up to a gas station. And all of a sudden four attendants swarm all over the car. One of them is giving her gas, one is wiping her windshield, one is checking her tires, and one is checking the oil. But a fifth attendant just looks on with a smile.

So one of the attendants stops and asks him, "Aren't you coming over to check something?" And the guy says, "I don't have to, I'm her husband!"

☆ ☆ ☆ ☆ ☆

Good cook: That good ol' woman could make a rip-snortin' meal out'n a bone's smell.

☆ ☆ ☆ ☆ ☆

An eighty-year-old widowed grandfather surprises everyone at Sunday dinner over at his granddaughter's when he shows up with his new bride, a petite redhead.

When everyone at the table learns that the new bride is just nineteen, they explode with astonishment and, bewildered, they take the elderly gentleman aside and say, "Grandfather, how could you do something so outrageous as this? Marrying a nineteen-year-old girl? You're over eighty. Do you realize that sex with a young girl like that at your age could be fatal?"

And the old man looks at them and says, "If she dies, she dies -- I'll get another one!"

☆ ☆ ☆ ☆ ☆

Contentment is when your earning power equals your yearning power.

☆ ☆ ☆ ☆ ☆

Annabelle should never have married Peter. She just is not a sincere, true person. You see, she married Peter while she was engaged to George so she could have a secret place to meet Eddie and make Bill jealous in front of Al.

74

"WELL, WAKE HIM!"

Said an ardent young bridegroom named Trask,
"I will grant any boon that you ask."
    Said the bride, "Kiss me, dearie,
    Until I grow weary,"
But he died of old age at the task.

Carolyn Wells

☆ ☆ ☆ ☆ ☆

Arkansas buggy: A wheel barrow.

☆ ☆ ☆ ☆ ☆

Sam accused his wife of being unable to keep a secret. She replied that wasn't so, that she could keep a secret just fine. The problem was with the people she told the secret to, not her.

☆ ☆ ☆ ☆ ☆

Poor cook: That woman cain't cook worth a dern. Why she'd scorch water tryin' to boil it.

In the waiting room of a fitness club, the management displayed this poster, titled, "Are you ready for our services?"
1. Have you burnt out more than two refrigerator bulbs in the last month?
2. On your recent cruise down the coast of Florida, did the captain request that you remain in the center of the boat?
3. On your last stop at the window of a fast-food drive-thru restaurant, were more than four waiters needed to deliver your order?

☆ ☆ ☆ ☆ ☆

She constantly complained that he never gave her anything, never a gift or present or surprise. So he surprised her with a gift of a girdle. "That ought to hold you," he said.

☆ ☆ ☆ ☆ ☆

They were talking about a product that, if taken regularly, reduces a man's sexual urge. "I don't see anything so derned unusual about that," one fellow responded. "Heck fire, I married one forty years ago."

☆ ☆ ☆ ☆ ☆

"As I understand you," the marriage counselor said, "you want a divorce. Yet you refuse to tell me why."

"Believe me, counselor, I sure as heck have my reasons."

"That may be, but I don't get it. After all, your wife is lovely, gentle, kind and beautiful, with a lovely figure. I cannot for the life of me figure why you want a divorce."

The fellow removed his shoe, then said, "Consider this shoe, counselor, the leather is excellent, quite handsome, right?" The counselor nodded his head. "It is beautifully made, good to look at and well-proportioned."

"I'm not sure what you are getting at," the counselor admitted. "Could you explain?"

"Sure. To an outsider, this shoe is great in every way but ... but I'm the only one who knows that it pinches."

☆ ☆ ☆ ☆ ☆

Then there was the prolific woman who had eleven kids, then quit! When asked why she didn't go ahead and make it an even dozen, she replied, "No! It would interfere with my career!"

76

"Jimmy Peters has his heart set on marrying the widow Rogers," Ella Fitzgerald told her friend. "He asked her last night."

"He did? Now that is surprising."

"Yep. He asked if he could take her husband's place."

"And what'd she say?"

"She said it was OK with her. All he had to do was make arrangements with the undertaker."

☆ ☆ ☆ ☆ ☆

It is hard to meet a man who would not rather be the second husband of a widow than her first.

☆ ☆ ☆ ☆ ☆

Mary Summers made a fortune off the story she made up.

"Wonderful! Who'd she manage to sell it to?"

"The jury!"

☆ ☆ ☆ ☆ ☆

Finally, after years of an unsatisfactory marriage, Edna decided to get a divorce. It was his failure to give her fun that was more than she could take. She said to her husband, "Harry, if you don't give me the money to buy some new clothing, I'm sure as heck gonna go outside stone-naked and run around the neighborhood just...like...that! And then you can guess what the neighbors'll think of you after **that**?"

And Harry replied, "I'd guess they'd say I married you for your money."

☆ ☆ ☆ ☆ ☆

Nutty wife: She's got a set of dishes, all right, but it's a few plates short of full!

☆ ☆ ☆ ☆ ☆

They tell the story about a married woman who caught a peeping Tom and almost killed the guy before her husband pulled her off him.

"I don't blame her," his friend said after hearing the story. "She must have been mad as hell having a guy spy on her like that."

"Well, it wasn't the spying on her that got her so made at him."

"No? Then what was her problem?"

"The jerk tried to reach in and pull the curtains shut!"

" WHOA! WHAT EVER HAPPENED TO 'OBEY'? "

Plastic surgery is becoming more and more common. They tell the story of a woman who felt she was losing her husband even though she had had several facelifts. When she appeared before her physician, she confessed, "Doctor, I have something I didn't bargain on."

"And what is that?" the physician asked.

"That dimple on my chin. I didn't bargain on that, Doctor."

"That's not a dimple, Madam," the doctor told her. "It's your navel."

☆ ☆ ☆ ☆ ☆

Wasteful housewife: That woman is plain wasteful. She's more wasteful than a busload of lawyers going over a cliff and three seats empty.

☆ ☆ ☆ ☆ ☆

His wife is so derned pretty that she could make a glass eye blink.

Then there's the story of the man and wife out raking leaves from their front lawn. Suddenly the wife dropped her rake, walked to her husband and kicked him in the shins.

"Why'd you do that?" he yelled.

"Because you're such a lousy lover, that's why!" she shouted back.

As she was walking away, he ran up to her and kicked her in the rear end. She turned around and snarled, "What was that for?"

"For knowing the difference!"

☆ ☆ ☆ ☆ ☆

Description of a good wife: Why that wife of mine is some punkins...I wouldn't trade her off for twenty acres of red hogs.

☆ ☆ ☆ ☆ ☆

Did you hear the one about the woman whose husband was rapidly becoming an alcoholic? She decided to use a recommended cure. She dressed up like the devil and hid behind a tree so as to meet him on his drunk and staggering way home from work. When hubby came by, she confronted him, dressed in her red outfit, long horns, red tail and pitchfork.

"Who in hell are y-you?" the hubby stammered.

"The devil you drunkard! The devil, that's who!"

"Well, fer goodness shakes, Buddy, c'mon home, I married y-y-your shister."

☆ ☆ ☆ ☆ ☆

George Edmonds came out of his workroom into the kitchen utterly furious about a particular bill. "How come," he said, "that the funeral parlor sends me a bill for sixty dollars? Why, I paid them a thousand over six months ago. And here's another bill for sixty dollars! Every...blamed...month, I get a bill for sixty dollars..."

"That's the charge for Uncle Peter's funeral, you know," his wife replied.

"As I said, I paid them over six months ago! So why this additional sixty bucks?"

"You know, dear, that poor Uncle Peter didn't have a decent suit to his name. So I rented him one."

☆ ☆ ☆ ☆ ☆

It seems more fitting today to say of a woman, "She's not getting a divorce, she's merely being recycled."

Blind dates seldom lead to marriage. Edna Jones has lots of stories about male losers. One young lad showed up and complained, "Gee, Edith, my collar's awful tight."

She looked at him and said, "Well, no wonder, you've got your head through the buttonhole."

Then she looked down at his feet and saw that he was wearing one white shoe and one black one. Both were brand new. She said to him, "Where'd you get that pair of shoes? They don't match."

"Well, that's right," he said, "and you know, I got another pair at home just like them."

☆ ☆ ☆ ☆ ☆

And then there are the rural big drinkers. One swain took a load out at the lake and got pretty drunk, so his friends unhooked his team and left him in his own wagon.

The next morning he woke up and said, "Boy, I've either lost a damn good team or found a damn good wagon."

☆ ☆ ☆ ☆ ☆

There's a flood in a little Ohio town and two teenagers are sitting on top of a house.

As they sit there watching different articles floating along the water, they notice a derby hat float by. Pretty soon the hat turns and comes back and then it turns again and goes downstream. After it goes some distance, it again turns around and comes back.

So the girl says, "Do you see that derby? First it goes downstream. And then it turns and comes back."

And the boy replies, "Oh, that's my old man. This morning he said come hell or high water, he was going to cut the grass."

☆ ☆ ☆ ☆ ☆

Ugly wife: She's so derned homely that her husband takes her picture when he goes drinkin' so he'll know to stop drinkin' when she appears to be good-lookin'.

☆ ☆ ☆ ☆ ☆

Bigamy is one way of avoiding the painful publicity of divorce and the expense of alimony.

Oliver Herford

In New York, there are marriage-arrangers, men and women who are given the needs of the family and who then go out and seek a suitable mate. The marital arranger also may be called directly by a man or woman seeking a mate for themselves. In this case, a middle-aged fellow contracted with the marriage-arranger.

Soon the bachelor got a call to come visit a "great prospect, superb woman" for his marriage.

The arranger and the bachelor met at the woman's house. After brief introductions, the bachelor pulled the arranger to one side and said, "What have you done! Why ask me to submit to this! She's old, ugly, she squints, smells, has terrible teeth, bleary eyes, and that breath...ugh!"

"You can talk louder," the marriage-arranger said, "she's deaf too."

☆ ☆ ☆ ☆ ☆

Tommy Manville described alimony this way: "She cried and the judge wiped her tears with my checkbook."

☆ ☆ ☆ ☆ ☆

That wife of his is so stupid that she'd have to have an owner's manual to try on a pair of shoes.

"I'm on a seafood diet, when I see food I eat it."

When asked why he took so much abuse from his political opponents without hitting back with the same tactics, Abraham Lincoln remarked, "I feel a good deal as a man whom I will call 'Jones,' whom I once knew, did about his wife. He was one of your meek men, and had the reputation of being badly hen-pecked. At last, one day, his wife was seen switching him out of the house. A day or two afterwards, a man met him in the street and said: 'Jones, I have always stood up for you, as you know; but I am not going to do it any longer. Any man who will stand quietly and take a switching from his wife deserves to be horse-whipped.'

"Jones looked up with a wink, patting his friend on the back, 'Now don't,' said he, 'why it didn't hurt me any and you've no idea what a power of good it did Sarah Ann!'"

☆ ☆ ☆ ☆ ☆

The wife of an Ozark mountain man suddenly lost her mind and was hauled off in an ambulance to a nearby mental hospital. An attendant stayed behind to get all necessary data from the husband, who wailed, "Now what in heck do you reckon couda gone wrong with that woman? Why, fer gosh sakes, she ain't been out'n the kitchen fer the last twenty years."

☆ ☆ ☆ ☆ ☆

Back in the good old days of hillbilly jokes, they told this one about the farm couple who came to town once a week to stock up on groceries. The farmer rode a mule while the wife walked behind him carrying the groceries.

Curious about this, the owner of the store asked the husband, "How come you ride the mule and yore wife she walks behind you?"

"Well," the farmer said, "'see, my wife, she ain't got no mule."

☆ ☆ ☆ ☆ ☆

Wife with a cute figure: Man she's built like a brick outhouse. I mean...nothin' would look mighty good on her.

☆ ☆ ☆ ☆ ☆

Edith was fed up with her husband, Jimmy. One evening, after a long quarrel, she said, "Get out of this house. Now! I never want to see you again. Go!"

Jimmy was silent a moment, then said, "All right, but I have one request to make before I go."

"And what is it?"

"Before I go, would you mind getting off my lap?"

Mary Ernest's husband was wild and woolly. He loved to drink and gamble, and he was rarely home before dawn. His wife gave him holy heck every chance she got, berating him about wasting all their money and depriving the children and all that. But it didn't do a bit of good.

So one day her friend, Nelly Sachs, suggested a new tactic. "Try a different way," Nelly suggested, "use a bit of psychology on him. Remember, you can catch more flies with honey than with vinegar."

Mary agreed to try it. The next time her husband came in late, she said, "Hello, Dearie. Come right on in to me." Now the old boy was startled, looked at her with wide-open eyes and came into the room. "Take this comfy chair here," she said, "and I'll fetch you a bite to eat." She went to the kitchen, then returned with a lovely snack plate for him. As he finished eating, she snuggled up to him and said, "Honey, sweetheart, dearest, let's you and I go to the bedroom."

The old boy shook his head slowly, saying, "Might just as well, I guess, 'cause I'm sure as heck goin' to catch hell when I get home anyway."

☆ ☆ ☆ ☆ ☆

Promiscuous woman: They say the only time she'll sleep alone was when her tombstone reads: "She sleeps alone."

☆ ☆ ☆ ☆ ☆

Barbara Walters asked Robert Mitchum what made his marriage work now that he had been married forty-two years. Mitchum replied, "Lack of imagination, I suppose."

☆ ☆ ☆ ☆ ☆

"I've heard that your wife came from an old, distinguished Chicago family."
"Not precisely 'came,' You see, she brought it with her."

☆ ☆ ☆ ☆ ☆

Most men don't know the value of a woman's love...until they start paying alimony.

☆ ☆ ☆ ☆ ☆

When Jenny Flinders asked her husband if she looked fifty, he replied, "Honey, you sure as heck don't...but you used to."

Two farmers were having coffee in the town's restaurant. One asked the other, "Bill, what do you think of Pete's new wife?"

"Heck fire," Bill exclaimed, "I coulda shut mah eyes, then reached out and touched somethin' a heluva lot better."

☆ ☆ ☆ ☆ ☆

The parishioner brought his difficulties to the preacher. "I'm really ashamed to tell you this, Parson, but I want to divorce my wife."

"You ought to be ashamed," the Parson stormed. "A good man would not think of such a thing. And you, of all people, disappoint me. You know that the readings say, 'When a man divorceth his wife not only the angels but the very stones weepeth.'"

"True enough, Parson, but all that is their business. As for me, I wanteth to singeth a songeth of joyeth."

☆ ☆ ☆ ☆ ☆

"My wife has been attending the Gaffigan Adult School of Cooking," Brian O'Brian told his friend.

"Is she cooking much better now?" his friend asked.

"I should say so! Both of us now truly appreciate nourishing, tasty, restaurant food."

" ANOTHER IRRITATING THING, SHE ALWAYS HAS TO HAVE THE LAST...."

Farmer Bill Edwins noticed his hired man start out to call on his girlfriend and carrying a flashlight to see the way.

"You young fellers are sure puny," Bill told the hired man. "Why, when I was a young feller and went to see my girl, I never carried no light atall."

"Sure," the hired man said while he began to run, "and look what you got."

Have you noticed that you no longer hear about men who hide behind a woman's skirt. Sure not hard to figure out the reason why.

☆ ☆ ☆ ☆ ☆

There's a great story told up in New England and it's centered around the small town country store. It seems that half a dozen old guys were sitting around the stove on a winter's morning when an old gal entered, a friend to them all, and said, "I want to buy a mouse trap. Last night a mouse got into my drawers and chewed all the fringe off my center piece."

Naturally, the men all began to snicker, then to roar with laughter while the old girl stood there looking at them as if they were insane, or drunk. The old girl paid for her purchase and left, shaking her head in disgust at those drunken bums around the stove and she never suspected that she had created an imperishable story about herself.

☆ ☆ ☆ ☆ ☆

If a woman complains about the man she married, it just could be that she could have caught a bigger, tastier fish if she'd had better bait.

☆ ☆ ☆ ☆ ☆

Forty years ago, J. W. Cunnigham asserted his male rights when he wrote, "It's about time for some courageous male to stand up on his hind legs and start a movement for masculine rights -- and one of his first reforms will be to change all those signs that say 'LADIES' and 'MEN' to read 'WOMEN' and 'GENTLEMEN.'"

☆ ☆ ☆ ☆ ☆

Have you noticed how there is behind every successful man, a mother-in-law who always said he'd never make good.

Hank's wife was a terrible shrew, always scolding him. One day, in his frontier community, a boy ran up to him and screamed, "A cougar done got in yore house and yore wife's the only one t'home."

Hank just stood there as if he hadn't heard.

"Ain't y gonna do nothin' about that cougar?" the boy wailed.

"Nope," Hank answered. "That cougar went in thar of his own blamed free will and he'll just have to look out for hisself as best he kin!"

☆ ☆ ☆ ☆ ☆

There is something magical about the fact that success almost always comes faster to the guy your wife almost married.

☆ ☆ ☆ ☆ ☆

"Before I married my wife," Pete Frazee said, "it was nothing but wine, women and song. Now that I'm her husband, it's beer, mama and TV."

☆ ☆ ☆ ☆ ☆

Private Ernest Masters made an emergency request to see his commanding officer. He was granted permission.

"Colonel, Sir," he said, "I have got to get a three-day pass."

"State your reasons, Private."

"It's like this, Sir. My wife is in service, too. And she's just been promoted to sergeant. So, you see, now I have that rare opportunity to do what every soldier has dreamed of doing throughout the last 100 years."

☆ ☆ ☆ ☆ ☆

All men are born free and equal, but then lots of them grow up and get married.

☆ ☆ ☆ ☆ ☆

Mary Simpkins went to join her husband at the park. She stood waiting for the bus to take her there. And she had her little dog on a leash beside her.

The bus stopped. "Lady," the bus driver said, "don't you know you can't ride the bus with that dog?"

"Oh, is that so! Well, you know what you can do with your damned bus, don't you?"

"Sure do, lady. And if you do the same with your dog, you can ride on my bus."

"HON, WHEN YOU MOW BY THE HOUSE WOULD YOU GET ME A GLASS OF LEMONADE?"

"I'm sure upset," Bill Jones told his friend, Bob. "My wife says she'll leave me, just walk out of the house if I don't stop running around."

"Gee, that's tough," said Bob.

"It sure as heck is. I'm really going to miss her."

You know the honeymoon is over when the husband takes his wife off that precious pedestal and puts her on a budget.

A near-sighted fellow named Coulter
Led a glamorized gal to the altour.
 Quite lovely he thought her
 Till some strong soap and hot water
Made her look like the rock of Gibralter.

The marriage counselor offered this advice to the fellow who came to see him about his overbearing wife: "The best way to cure your wife of constant nagging is to show her affection, understanding, abiding care...and stuffing a pair of old socks in her mouth."

☆ ☆ ☆ ☆ ☆

The Couples Club met once a month just for fun. At one such meeting, the subject was marriage and each couple was to tell how they first met. The Joneses, Bob and Marie, were called on first. "And how did you meet your wife?" Bob was asked.

"Folks, I didn't actually meet her," Bob responded. "She overtook me."

Another couple, Peter and Pauline Welch, were next. The question: "Peter, is your wife careful with the family budget? Frugal?"

"She sure is," Peter responded, "why on her fortieth birthday, she saved by using only twenty-eight candles."

☆ ☆ ☆ ☆ ☆

"My marriage is happy," a long-married fellow once said, "because I can make my wife do anything she wants to do."

☆ ☆ ☆ ☆ ☆

She's so prone to divorce that her towels are labeled, His, Hers and Next.

☆ ☆ ☆ ☆ ☆

Eddie Versace came home weeping bitterly. He had gone to propose to his girl and his father eagerly awaited her response. "So what happened, Eddie?" the old man asked. "Did she accept?"

"Oh, Dad, she sure didn't. When I told her what you advised me to do, she slapped my face and sent me home."

"Did you start out by saying what I told you to, what I told your mother when she accepted my proposal? 'Dear, time stands still when I look in your eyes.' Did you say that?"

"Holy smokes, Dad. I got it wrong. I said, 'My dear, your face would stop a clock!'"

☆ ☆ ☆ ☆ ☆

Bertha is the talker in that family. She's always at it. But husband Bert doesn't mind. He's given her the best ears of his life.

Here's mighty good advice for husbands:
    To keep your marriage brimming,
    With love in the wedding cup,
    Whenever you're wrong, admit it,
    Whenever you're right, shut up.
        Ogden Nash, *"Marriage Lines,"* Little Brown & Co., 1964.

It was their 25th wedding anniversary but husband Tom seemed to have forgotten. Briefcase in hand, he started out the door.

"Haven't you forgotten what day this is?" his wife asked.

"Nope!"

"Well, gosh," she said, "let's celebrate, let's go do something unusual."

"OK by me," Tom said. "How about observing three minutes of silence?"

They have a good marriage because he always lets her have the last word. In fact, he lets her have the last three thousand words.

☆ ☆ ☆ ☆ ☆

"My wife is one heckuva great house cleaner. She really takes care of my things, too. She's so diligent about the house that she gets all my shirts wonderfully white...even the brown ones."

☆ ☆ ☆ ☆ ☆

Marie Blester was complaining that Elmer, her husband, never brought gifts home to her as he did before they were married. "You don't even bring me sweet rolls or a box of candy or anything at all as you used to do before we were married."

"I'm sorry about that, Dear," husband Elmer replied. "But you've got to realize, honey, that a man's a damn fool if he feeds worms to a fish after he's caught it"!

☆ ☆ ☆ ☆ ☆

Then there was the wife who divorced her husband for religious reasons. She really worshipped money and he...he didn't have any.

No woman marries for money; they are all clever enough, before marrying a millionaire, to fall in love with him first.

Cesare Pavese

☆ ☆ ☆ ☆ ☆

Then there was the Arkansas backwoods family with a huge number of children that kept the father busy working night and day. Finally, he made up his mind to take off alone for a week of rest. But his wife was upset, "You ain't got no feelin's fer me atall, Jake," she moaned. "Else you sho' wouldn't leave me heah with all them kids and no man to help. Why, we ain't got hardly a stick of wood fer the stove."

"Well, woman," the man declared, "I ain't takin' the axe with me."

☆ ☆ ☆ ☆ ☆

Two Kentucky hillbillies happened to meet in town. "How're thangs with y'all, Pete?" one asked.

"Not bad atall," Pete replied. "My old woman ain't talkin' to me thiseyer week...and I ain't in no mood to interrupt her."

"WHY DON'T YOU EVER SAY IT WITH FLOWERS, FRED?"

In the blithe days of honeymoon,
With Kate's allurements smitten,
I lov'd her late, I lov'd her soon,
And call'd her dearest kitten.

But now my kitten's grown a cat,
And cross like other wives.
O! By my soul my honest Mat,
I fear she has nine lives.

A quotation from James Boswell's *Life of Johnson*

"Terry, I hear your wife has been running around again. If she were mine, I'd shoot her."
"You'd need a machine gun."

Wife: "I remember a time when you were plumb crazy to marry me, Harry."
Harry: "So do I. But I just didn't realize it at the time."

Man is a natural polygamist: He always has one woman leading him by the nose and another hanging on to his coattails.

H. L. Mencken

☆ ☆ ☆ ☆ ☆

The bridegroom was in a poetic mood at the seaside resort: "Roll on, though lovely, stirring, deep blue ocean. Roll, roll, roll on."
The bride hugged him tight, saying: "You are marvelous, Sweetie. And look! It's doing it!"

☆ ☆ ☆ ☆ ☆

They pulled Doris and Jimmy Bucarina out of their wrecked car and, as soon as he had caught his breath, he explained the bad accident. "You see," he gasped, "I taught my wife Doris how to drive the car but I never did explain how to aim it."

☆ ☆ ☆ ☆ ☆

When hubby offers to give mother-in-law a Jaguar for Christmas, it is just as well for the wife to be certain it doesn't have four legs.

Eddie Dukin had just retired and was enjoying the mere observation of the world instead of trying to make a living out of it. He and his wife were walking down the street at noon hour and many young ladies passed them. Eddie looked them all over, then said, "What will the short skirt be up to next."

Both admit that they are always having words! But he complains that they're always hers.

David: "I find it hard to believe that you always have the last word with your wife when I hear her continually ordering you here and there. And you go!"
"That is so, my friend. But, still...you notice that I have the last word. I always say, 'All right, Dear.'"

Both Harry and Selma wear pants, but it's easy to tell them apart. Harry is the one who listens.

"Sorry to keep you waiting so long," she said, coming down the stairs an hour late.
"Not to worry, Dear. I wasn't waiting, I was sojourning."

Pete Rosen wasn't sure just how to take his buddy's response to his question, "Does your wife like to do housework?"
Buddy's response was: "She likes to do nothing better."

Down in Arkansas, they say that custom has changed little. Many a man still sleeps with a battle-axe by his side.

Two old friends met for the first time in several years. They had a good talk and one asked, "Is your wife still as pretty as ever?"
"She sure is," the other replied. "It just takes her longer."

"WHAT'S-HER-NAME, HERE, SAYS I DON'T TREAT HER WITH ENOUGH RESPECT."

The newlyweds came walking down the gangplank of the plane that had brought them home from their honeymoon. "Honey," the bride said, "let's not act as if we were newlyweds. Let's try to appear as if we'd been married a long time."

"OK by me, Honey. You carry the suitcases."

☆ ☆ ☆ ☆ ☆

"What's the very best, the most favorable month in which to get married?"

"Septoctuary."

"Crazy, man. There's no such month."

"You got it right, man."

☆ ☆ ☆ ☆ ☆

Art Solon said he never knew what contentment, happiness, fulfillment meant until he married. But now he finds it's too late.

It is a truism that the ministerial associations frown upon all forms of gambling...except marriage.

Satan held up a restraining hand to the new arrival. "Just one second, Mister," the devil restrained him. "You're acting like you own this place."

"I sure as heck do, Satan. My wife has been giving it to me for years."

☆ ☆ ☆ ☆ ☆

It is next to impossible for a man to make a fool out of himself and not know it...especially if he's married.

☆ ☆ ☆ ☆ ☆

Mary Swanson had presented her husband with triplets. When she told him the good news, he replied, in his oafish way, "Mary, you're at it again. You just never quit exaggerating."

☆ ☆ ☆ ☆ ☆

Choose a wife rather by your ear than your eye.
Thomas Fuller, 1732

☆ ☆ ☆ ☆ ☆

Isn't it true that before your marriage, you, the man, would lie awake half the night worrying about something the sweet thing had said? But after you got married, you fall asleep before the misses had got half through saying it!

☆ ☆ ☆ ☆ ☆

When Dick Felten finally got around to making his will, he had the first line read: "Finally, I get to open my mouth!"

☆ ☆ ☆ ☆ ☆

A lady with manner superior
sought a divorce from her hubby inferior.
    And her grounds were that once,
    She had yelled at him, "Dunce!"
And he yelled, "Quiet, you horse's posterior."

A supposedly confirmed bachelor finally married. And the woman he married was a surprise to his friends because she was known to have a terrible disposition, to be argumentative to a fault, a genuine shrew. When asked why he picked this particular woman, he replied, "I did it for penance. I had too many dissipated years, drinking and whoorin' and such. I was afeared I'd not go to heaven unless I had some sufferin' here on earth. And my wife sure is bringin' it to me!"

A gossip ran into his wife and told her what her husband had said. Well, his wife blew her stack, saying she'd not be the means to get him into heaven, no siree.

And do you know, she turned around and became a wonderfully sweet-tempered, kind and considerate woman...a genuine model wife! Now THAT'S getting even!

☆ ☆ ☆ ☆ ☆

Did you hear about the girl who was six months pregnant? She wrote her boss a letter of resignation: "Dear Sir, I'm getting far too big for this job."

☆ ☆ ☆ ☆ ☆

Tad and Margie need to get some help around the house. Why, at the end of the day, Margie is so tired she can hardly keep her mouth open.

☆ ☆ ☆ ☆ ☆

Sam complains that he has several mouths to feed, and one very big one that he listens to.

☆ ☆ ☆ ☆ ☆

"I ain't ready to get married," Sam Rush told his buddy, Joe. "But, when I do, I want a gal who's an economist in the kitchen, a sweet lady when we got company and a fireball in the bedroom."

Well, time passed and Sam did get married. One day he again ran into Joe.

"How's life with you, Sam?" Joe asked.

"Fine and dandy, Joe. I done got myself hitched."

"Great! And is she just like the gal you described to me?"

"Not exactly. I sure enough did get all the qualities in my wife that I wanted. But they came a little bit mixed. Jenny's a fireball in the kitchen, a sweet lady when we got company, but she's an economist in the bedroom."

Husbands are like burning wood in your fireplace. If unattended, they go out.

☆ ☆ ☆ ☆ ☆

Terry Anderson, a salesman, had been on the road for several days. One morning, at his hotel, for breakfast, he ordered two eggs, very hard. "Then you can bring me two pieces of burnt toast and a cup of very weak and lukewarm coffee," he said.

The waitress didn't know what to make of the order: "Do you really want that, burnt toast and all?" she asked.

"Yep! Just that," he replied.

When the disconcerted waitress brought the odd meal to him, he invited her to sit down. "Now I'd like to have you sit and nag me," he told her, "I'm terribly homesick."

☆ ☆ ☆ ☆ ☆

The phone rang and Paul answered it, then called to his wife, "Sweetheart, come to the phone...somebody wants to listen to you."

"ANY TIME I ASK HIM TO DO ANYTHING AROUND THE HOUSE, HE ALWAYS HAS THE SAME RESPONSE."

The man showed his wife's injured hand to the doctor. "She did it getting dinner ready last night," he said, "I suspect it's frostbite."

☆ ☆ ☆ ☆ ☆

Husbands and wives from Texas do not underestimate themselves. Consider Pecos Bill. He had a horse so fierce that only he could ride it. So he forbade his wife, Slufoot Sue, to mount his horse. Naturally, being Texan and independent as are all Texan women, she determined to ride that horse...and did, bustle and all. She mounted Bill's horse and proceeded to stay on for about two minutes. Then she got thrown sky-high, coming down on her bustle whence she bounced sky-high again...and again...and again. She bounced so high for so long that they had to shoot her to keep her from starving to death.

☆ ☆ ☆ ☆ ☆

Ethel had laryngitis once and it was as if the phone was disconnected.

☆ ☆ ☆ ☆ ☆

A lawyer was explaining to the court that his witness was not necessarily unreliable just because he changed a statement he had previously made. "Consider this example," the lawyer said, "when I got here this morning I could have sworn that I had my Rolex watch with me. But, as a matter of fact, I left it home on the bathroom shelf."

That evening, arriving home, his wife said, "You sure went to a lot of trouble, sending that guy around for your watch. Did you really need it that bad?"

"I sent no one here for my Rolex!" he husband exploded. "I hope you didn't give it to him."

"I sure did," his wife replied. "Because he knew exactly where it was."

☆ ☆ ☆ ☆ ☆

They call her Tonsillitis, she's such a terrible pain in the neck.

☆ ☆ ☆ ☆ ☆

Some wives are forever fussy. Consider Peter Brown's wife. The other night, Pete got up out of bed to get a bite to eat and when he got back to the room, the bed was made.

Peggy Jones died and when she arrived at the Pearlies, she asked, "Is my husband here? His name is Jones."

"We have a lot of Joneses here," the angel replied, "please identify further."

"Jimmy Jones is his name."

"But we have many, many Jimmy Joneses here."

"Hm-m-m. Let's see. Oh, yes. He told me when he died if ever I was unfaithful to him, he'd turn over in his grave. Does that help?"

"You bet. Now I know that you mean Pinwheel Jones!"

Today, the high divorce rate would seem to indicate that women have not as yet made up their minds whether to have a man for a hubby or hobby.

☆ ☆ ☆ ☆ ☆

"Tell me, Grandma, when you and Grandpa had your first child, did Grandpa ever get up at night and handle the feeding of the baby?"

"No, he always left that up to me."

"I guess that was before women's lib, right?"

"No, it was before baby bottles!"

☆ ☆ ☆ ☆ ☆

Two women were discussing the problems with their marriages. "I know one thing, for sure!" one said. "I'm going to get a divorce."

"But why?"

"I saw that jerk I call my husband, going into a movie with another woman."

"Did you know who she was?"

"Never saw her before, in all my life."

"Well, did you ever stop to consider whether there could be an innocent explanation of it all? How come you didn't follow them into the theatre and find out?"

"Well, y'see, the fellow I was with had already seen the picture."

☆ ☆ ☆ ☆ ☆

If your child asks how Santa Claus gets into the house, just tell him he comes in through a large hole in daddy's wallet.

"HE COACHES THE LITTLE LEAGUE TEAM."

As most Americans know, a farmer with a prize bull or boar or stallion charges a fee for servicing the females of his breed. Now it so happened that a man stopped at the home of a farmer who had a prize bull. The man knocked at the door and it was opened by a young lady. "Could I speak with your father?" the stranger asked.

"Papa's out in the field," she replied, "but I handle his business when he's away. So if you want to breed your cow to our bull, Billy Jo, it'll cost you two hundred dollars."

"No, no, it's nothing like that. It's about your brother, Tom. He's been sparking my daughter and I just figured that your Pa and I ought to talk."

"Oh, that's a hoss of another color," the girl said. "Maybe you best go on back to the field and talk to my Pa. I don't what he charges for Tom."

☆ ☆ ☆ ☆ ☆

Rita Mae Brown must have been a tad discouraged when she wrote: "If the world were a logical place, men would ride side-saddle."

THE IDEAL HUSBAND TO HIS WIFE

We've lived for forty years, dear wife,
    And walked together side by side,
And you to-day are just as dear
    As when you were my bride.
I've tried to make life glad for you,
    One long, sweet honeymoon of joy,
A dream of marital content,
    Without the least alloy.
I've smoothed all boulders from our path,
    That we in peace might toil along,
By always hastening to admit
    That I was right and you were wrong.

No mad diversity of creed
    Has ever sundered me from thee;
For I permit you evermore
    To borrow your ideas of me.
And thus it is, through weal or woe,
    Our love forevermore endures;
For I permit that you should take
    My views and creeds and make them yours.
And thus I let you have my way,
    And thus in peace we toil along,
For I am willing to admit
    That I am right and you are wrong.

And when our matrimonial skiff
    Strikes snags in love's meandering stream,
I lift our shallop from the rocks,
    And float as in a placid dream.
And well I know our marriage bliss
    While life shall last will never cease;
For I shall always let thee do,
    In generous love, just what I please.
Peace comes, and discord flies away,
    Love's bright day follows hatred's night;
For I am ready to admit
    That you are wrong and I am right.
Sam Walter Foss

☆ ☆ ☆ ☆ ☆

Woman: A creature whom a man can't get along with or without. Animal usually living in the vicinity of man, and having a rudimentary susceptibility to domestication.

Ambrose Bierce

They have begun to call Ellen by a choice nickname, A.T.&T. because she's "Always Talking and Talking."

☆ ☆ ☆ ☆ ☆

It rarely occurs to teenagers that the day will come when they'll know as little as their parents.

☆ ☆ ☆ ☆ ☆

Mary Elwood had lost her husband some five or six years ago and was only beginning to get used to her widowhood when, one day, she was visited by a genie. He offered her three wishes.

To test the reality of the situation, she asked for a pail of diamonds--and instantly and on the floor before her, was a pail of diamonds. Convinced, she thought for a few moments, then asked to be made into a lovely, young blond. And she was.

For her last wish, she requested the genie to turn her old tomcat into a handsome, gracious and charming young man. And that, too, happened.

The young man stood before his blushing mistress and said, "Now, aren't you sorry that you had the vet neuter me?"

☆ ☆ ☆ ☆ ☆

Pregnant wife: She's done swallowed a blimp seed.

☆ ☆ ☆ ☆ ☆

There is no fairness between the way the world considers men and women. When he comes into the world, all ask, "And how is the mother getting along?" When he gets married, the only things you hear is, "What a lovely bride." and when he kicks the bucket, what do people say? "How much did he leave her?"

☆ ☆ ☆ ☆ ☆

Girdle: A device to keep a broad misfortune from spreading.

☆ ☆ ☆ ☆ ☆

His grade school son studying geography, asked, "What do you call those folks who wear rings in their noses and are used as beasts of burden?"

"Husbands," his dad replied.

101

The 75-year-old groom, with the young wife, caused a lot of attention as he checked into the resort hotel. The following morning, the old boy came strutting into the dining room, lookin' great with a big smile on his face. He proceeded to order an enormous breakfast. He laughed and joked and was in obvious good spirits, whereas his young wife, who came into the room a half hour later, looked worn out. She ordered coffee in a voice so weak the waiter had to ask her to repeat the order.

The old man finished his breakfast, excused himself and left for their room. This gave the waitress a chance to ask the bride, "Honey, I can't figure it out. That old geezer, your husband, looks like a million and you look like two cents. What's wrong?"

"That guy double-crossed me," the bride said. "He told me he'd saved up for fifty years! And all the time I thought he was talking about money!"

☆ ☆ ☆ ☆ ☆

Susie Edward's husband has feet so big that she says he has to put on his pants by pulling them over his head.

☆ ☆ ☆ ☆ ☆

Sandy Cooper got lucky at the crap table one night and won $5,000. He should have quit, but he didn't and proceeded to lose it all before the night had ended. The shock of it caused his death from a heart attack.

Sandy's friend, Jimmy Bucari, was picked to inform the widow. He found her in the kitchen baking a cake.

"Howdy, Mrs. Cooper," Jimmy said. "I came to tell you that Sandy shot craps most of last night and won $5,000. Isn't that great?"

"Oh, yes. Thanks for telling me... ."

"But," Jimmy interrupted her, "He bet it all on one throw of the dice and lost the entire five thousand bucks."

"Five thousand dollars shot to hell," Mrs. Cooper screamed. "He should drop dead!"

Jimmy took off his hat, saying, "He did, Ma'am. He did."

☆ ☆ ☆ ☆ ☆

Alimony: That's the same as buying corn for somebody else's cow.

A chap they all call Aloysius,
Of his wife and a guy grew suspysius.
   And quicker than you'd think
   He found them by the sink
But they were only doing the dysius.
He called his wife Echo because she always had to have the last word.

☆ ☆ ☆ ☆ ☆

An ideal wife is one who remains faithful to you but tries to be just as charming as if she weren't.

Sacha Guitry

☆ ☆ ☆ ☆ ☆

"I saw you and your wife at the beach last Sunday. When did she get that bikini?"
"The week before. But you know, when she wears it, it reminds me of twenty pounds of potatoes loaded in a ten pound sack."
"Yeah, and that reminds me of the new dress my wife bought last week. Fits her like a glove. Yep! She sticks out in five places."

☆ ☆ ☆ ☆ ☆

"Are you telling me that your wife ran off with your best friend?"
"I sure am."
"I wonder if I know him. What's his name?"
"Can't tell you. I never met the guy."

☆ ☆ ☆ ☆ ☆

Women's lib has definitely, without question, gone to excess when you hear the preacher say: "Let's all sing Number 38 in the Austerity **Her** Book."

☆ ☆ ☆ ☆ ☆

Sadie Converse was the worst shrew in the entire neighborhood. She screamed and alienated all the neighbors, reduced her husband to an overpowered hulk of "yes ma'ams," and made her dog and cat so upset that they ran away. But then she died. As the casket was lowered into the grave, there came a terrible thunderstorm with lightning and roaring thunder. "By God," said one of the mourners, "she's got there!"

"THERE, THERE, DEAR—WE ALL MAKE MISTAKES. JUST WHAT KIND OF A STUPID, IDIOTIC BLUNDER WAS IT?"

In early days, there were no lipstick flavors. When you kissed a girl, all you tasted was girl.

☆ ☆ ☆ ☆ ☆

A husband with twelve children promised himself that if his family had one more child, he'd go out and end his life by hanging. Well, lo and behold, his wife became pregnant and delivered herself of their thirteenth child. So the husband took a rope and headed for timber to find a tree. But he was soon seen walking back out of the woods toward his house. He told a friend what happened: "I got to thinking, just before I jumped off the topmost limb, noose around my neck, that I just might be hanging the wrong man."

☆ ☆ ☆ ☆ ☆

Paul Evers was about to leave for work when his wife pointed across the street and complained, "Every morning when our neighbor, Eddie Smith, leaves for the office, he kisses his wife good-bye. Now why don't **you** do that?"

"Me? Why I hardly know the woman!"

"Last week I got a wonderful bedroom suite for my wife."

"Yeah, my what a good trade."

☆ ☆ ☆ ☆ ☆

Charlie Shuck went to see his attorney to make a will. When it was all done, he told the lawyer that he wanted only one more thing added, that he wanted to be buried at sea.

"But why?" the lawyer asked.

"That's so my wife can be taken care of if she goes ahead with her threat to dance on my grave."

☆ ☆ ☆ ☆ ☆

Allan Mayer complained constantly of indigestion. His wife finally talked him into seeing their physician. Allan was told to drink a cup of hot water every morning. "Hell, Doctor," Allan exploded, "I've been doing that for thirty-five years. Only my wife calls it coffee!"

☆ ☆ ☆ ☆ ☆

The only thing that holds a marriage together is the husband bein' big enough to keep his mouth shut, to step back and see where his wife is wrong.

Archie Bunker

☆ ☆ ☆ ☆ ☆

A man waited impatiently outside a public telephone booth. The phone had been in use for at least ten minutes and the user merely stood inside, holding the receiver in his hand, saying not one word. "Hey, buddy," the impatient fellow said at last. "I need to use that phone for an important call. Would you please finish up, hang up and get out of there!"

"Just be patient," the other fellow said. "I'm having a conversation with my wife."

☆ ☆ ☆ ☆ ☆

George Peters says that his wife's bridge club indulges in lots of gossip. George calls it mouth-to-mouth recitation.

☆ ☆ ☆ ☆ ☆

At the end of his divorce proceedings, Tim Alshuler said, "that word, 'alimony' is merely a contraction of 'all-his-money'."

"I can tell from your talk that matrimony, to you, is a serious word."

"It's a heluva lot more than that. It's a sentence."

☆ ☆ ☆ ☆ ☆

A mother and her young daughter were forced to stand and await seats at the overcrowded theatre. Finally, the usher came and said, "Ma'am, I have two separate seats, would you like them?"

"Certainly not," she stormed. "Would you separate a mother from her daughter?"

"You are right as rain, Ma'am," he replied. "I did that once and I've regretted it ever since."

☆ ☆ ☆ ☆ ☆

Mamie Jenkins had been to an upscale dress shop and had on her new dress when hubby Al came in the door. "How do you like my new dress, Dear?" she asked.

"Swell," he said. "But I think you ought to get into it further, my dear."

☆ ☆ ☆ ☆ ☆

Most divorced men understand Ambrose Bierce's definition of litigation: *A machine which you go into as a pig and come out as a sausage.*

☆ ☆ ☆ ☆ ☆

"George, come and look at how I've arranged my birthday candles on this lovely cake. Isn't it stunning?"

"Sure is, your arrangement is great, but not your arithmetic!"

☆ ☆ ☆ ☆ ☆

Henry and Jim stood before a huge painting titled, "Lady Echo." Henry nodded and said, "Lovely, isn't it? But why do they depict an echo as woman?"

"Probably," guessed Jim, "because she always has the last word."

"Could be," Henry said, "but on the other hand, an echo only replies when spoken to."

"I've been unlucky two times in my marriages," Abe Martin said.
"That's tough, Abe. Do you want to tell me about it?"
"Well, my first wife ran away."
"And what happened with you and your second wife?"
"She stayed."

☆ ☆ ☆ ☆ ☆

"I've half a mind to get married."
"That's about all you'll need, Man."

☆ ☆ ☆ ☆ ☆

The lecturer, a dietitian, was addressing a large audience in Chicago. "The material we put into our stomach is enough to have killed most of us sitting here, years ago. Red meat is awful. Vegetables can be disastrous, and none of us realizes the germs in our drinking water. But there is one thing that is the most dangerous of all and we all of us eat it. Can anyone here tell me what lethal product I'm referring to? You, Sir, in the first row, please give us your idea."

The man lowered his hand and said, "Wedding cake."

**"DON'T INTERRUPT WHILE YOUR GRANDMOTHERS
BUTTING IN!"**

"Jasper, I'm really worried about our relationship. You don't speak sweetly and affectionately and lovingly to me. I think you have stopped loving me."

"Stopped loving you?" her husband replied. "That's ridiculous. I love you more than I ever did, more than I can tell you. More than life itself! Now shut up and let me read my paper."

☆ ☆ ☆ ☆ ☆

Talk about two-faced. Why, his wife is more like three-faced! She could sing a trio all by herself!

☆ ☆ ☆ ☆ ☆

Pedestrian: A man who has two cars, a wife and a daughter.

☆ ☆ ☆ ☆ ☆

"Quit bugging me about money," the wife exploded in anger. "I admit to it. I do love to spend money. But name me another **extravagance** I have!"

☆ ☆ ☆ ☆ ☆

Pat Finnegan had been taking an adult education course in French, and loving it. Too, he liked to show off his knowledge of the language every chance he got. So, one night when he got home from work, he opened the door and walked in the house to stand in front of his wife. He held out his arms, crooning to her: "Je t'adore."

"You lazy bum, you. Shut it yourself!"

☆ ☆ ☆ ☆ ☆

"I'll admit that I'm outspoken," the wife said. "You really mean that?" gasped her hubby. "By whom?"

☆ ☆ ☆ ☆ ☆

A few years back, a man was sleeping in the upper berth of a transcontinental train. But a persistent tapping from the bunk below kept awakening him. "What's going on down there?" he called. Receiving no reply, he leaned over the side of his upper and again called to the person below, "What's going on down there?"

"I'm cold," a lady's voice replied. "Would you be so kind as to get me a blanket?"

"Why don't we pretend we're married...that'd be even better, wouldn't it?" he asked.

"Great idea," she said, giggling.

"Good. Now go get your own damned blanket!"

"It is simply not true that I married a millionaire," Harriet Jones told her friend, "I made him one."

"And what was he before you married him?" her friend asked.

"A multi-millionaire," Harriet said.

☆ ☆ ☆ ☆ ☆

One can feel pity for the father of three kids in college. He tells his wife that they are getting poorer by degrees.

☆ ☆ ☆ ☆ ☆

A married couple got into a fight a few days ago. And the guy didn't see his wife for more than a week. But then things got better and he got so that he could see her a teenie weenie bit...out of one eye.

☆ ☆ ☆ ☆ ☆

When you see the kind of women some men marry, you realize that these guys must really hate to make their own breakfast and bed.

☆ ☆ ☆ ☆ ☆

A woman went to an attorney, seeking advice on a divorce.

"Do you have grounds, Madam?" the lawyer asked.

"Oh yes. More than I need. I have over five acres."

"I guess you didn't understand my question. Let me put it another way. Do you have a grudge?"

"No, but we have a parking space," she replied.

"I'll try to be more explicit, Ma'am," said the attorney. "Does your husband beat you up?"

"No, usually I get up long before he does."

Losing patience, the attorney asked, "Are you quite sure, absolutely sure that you want a divorce?"

"I'm not the one who wants a divorce," she replied. "My husband does. He claims we don't communicate."

☆ ☆ ☆ ☆ ☆

Two men who hadn't seen each other in years, met on the street. In the course of their talk, trying to catch up on all those intervening years, one asked the other if he had married.

"Nope," the other replied. "I look this way because someone just spilled a cup of coffee on me."

109

" NOW, WHAT SEEMS TO BE THE TROUBLE WITH YOUR MARRIAGE?"

George and Pete were discussing their wives' reaction when they came home late last night. "I tell you, George," Pete said, "last night my wife got plumb historical when she met me at the door."

George corrected him: "I think you mean 'hysterical' don't you, Pete?"

"Nope, I mean just what I said, H-i-s-t-o-r-i-c-a-l. Why, she reminded me of stuff that happened between me and her forty years and more ago."

☆ ☆ ☆ ☆ ☆

There's a fellow in Nevada who has been married so many times that he now has the marriage license made out to "TO WHOM IT MAY CONCERN."

☆ ☆ ☆ ☆ ☆

The guy was bothering her and she was fed up with him, a total stranger. "Look, you wart, leave me alone. I don't want anything to do with you. You're old enough to be my father."

"That's very possible. What was your Mama's name?"

EXPERIENCE -- What a man gets in exchange for alimony.

Attorney Norm Jones looked up to see a badly beaten, almost crippled man entering his office. "You appear to be more in need of a doctor than a lawyer," Norm told him. "How can I help you?"

"Well, Sir," the man began, speaking with difficulty, "last night, I came home with beer on my breath and some lipstick smeared on my shirt collar and for no damned reason at all, my wife began to hit me with a baseball bat. Then, when she got tired, she called in her two brothers who live near us and they came over and beat me still more. Mr. Attorney, is that legal?"

"Yes. It is legal for her to beat you with a baseball bat. But...it is not legal for her to bring in pinch-hitters."

☆ ☆ ☆ ☆ ☆

"I think you are married to the most garrulous, talkative, gab-gab-gab woman in this entire world," Amos Pinkerton said to his friend, Adam.

"I suspect that you are right," Adam replied. "I've given that woman the very best ears of my life."

☆ ☆ ☆ ☆ ☆

I got our bank statement this morning,
The figures filled me with awe.
'Twas a standoff that might have been balanced,
But my wife was too quick on the draw!

☆ ☆ ☆ ☆ ☆

A novelist was furious with his editor for not catching a misprint in a proverb known to everyone. It seems that the editor printed it this way: "A word to the wife is sufficient."

☆ ☆ ☆ ☆ ☆

"My dear," said the husband at dinner, "I think it entirely unnecessary that you worship...truly worship me the way you've been doing lately."

"Why, Horace, whatever do you mean?"

"Well, my dear, for several days, you've been placing burnt offerings before me."

Ne'er take a wife till thou hast a house (and a fire) to put her in.
Benjamin Franklin

I accused my wife of taking all the change out of my pocket. She said she never knew that I had any change, and, secondly, that she never put her hands in my pockets in all of our married life, and in the third place, she said that the pocket where I said I had the change, why, that pocket had a hole in it.

☆ ☆ ☆ ☆ ☆

"I understand that you have a quiet uneventful life at home. How do you manage such things?"
"Well, my wife is our Secretary of the Treasury. Her mother is our Secretary of War and her father is our Secretary of the Interior..."
"And I expect that you are President. Right?"
"No, I'm the American taxpayer."

☆ ☆ ☆ ☆ ☆

"My wife is an angel," Terry Steinhauer remarked to his good friend, Eddy Zack. "You're sure lucky," Eddy replied. "Mine's still living."

☆ ☆ ☆ ☆ ☆

Fred Wassell looked up to see his mother-in-law walking toward the front of the house, carrying a broom. "Tell me," he said to her, "are you going to clean up with it or fly away on it?"

☆ ☆ ☆ ☆ ☆

There is a likely, unexpected and double price to pay for bigamy...two mothers-in-law.

☆ ☆ ☆ ☆ ☆

Dave Peterson's wife was spending half of her time at a health club and Dave was tired of it. "Look, dear," he said to her, "there's a simple way to improve your health. Simply eat what you don't want, drink what you don't like and do what you'd rather not. And you'll save money doin' it."

Marriage as defined by Herbert Spencer: "A ceremony in which rings are put on the finger of the lady and through the nose of the gentleman."

Harry Peters looked up from his checkbook in which he'd been writing for most of the evening and said to his wife, "Honey, I hope you'll remember this saying: 'What you don't owe won't hurt you.'"

☆ ☆ ☆ ☆ ☆

Here's a consolation for men: Perhaps you'll never be as great a man as your kids think you are, but neither will you be as big a fool as your mother-in-law thinks you are.

☆ ☆ ☆ ☆ ☆

Wife: "Criticize me all you want, Cliff, but you got to admit I have an open mind."
Husband: "I do agree. And a mouth to match."

☆ ☆ ☆ ☆ ☆

H. L. Mencken defines love as an emotion that is based on an opinion of women that is impossible for those who have had any experience with them.

☆ ☆ ☆ ☆ ☆

"Tom, wake up! You're talking in your sleep again. Stop it!"
"OK, I'll make a deal with you," Tom said sleepily. "You let me talk when I'm awake and I'll try to control myself when I'm sleeping."

☆ ☆ ☆ ☆ ☆

Definition of a wife: A woman who sticks by you through thick and thin, through all that woe and those troubles you'd never had if you hadn't married her in the first place.

☆ ☆ ☆ ☆ ☆

"My wife deserted me," groaned the unhappy fellow. "She up and ran off with my car and a traveling salesman."
"How awful," exclaimed his friend. "And it was a brand new car, too!"

Phil Gibbens had just concluded his fourth divorce. Asked why he kept on marrying, divorce after divorce, he replied, "Women are a problem for me. But they're a problem I like to wrestle with."

☆ ☆ ☆ ☆ ☆

The term "GENTLEMAN" is not heard much these days. So definition might be in order as follows:
A man who, when his wife drops her knitting, kicks it over to her so that she can easily pick it up.

A husband who steadies the stepladder so that his wife will not fall while she paints the ceiling.

☆ ☆ ☆ ☆ ☆

At breakfast, Ruth Elkins was having trouble explaining to her disinterested husband just why their budget for food was inadequate. Finally, exasperated, she screamed, "You're having trouble with your hearing, I presume!"
"Nope," he replied, "with my listening."

☆ ☆ ☆ ☆ ☆

Reba and Tom were riding the bus downtown. At a stop, two elderly ladies got aboard but there were no seats and they had to stand. "Why don't you get up and let one of those ladies sit down?" Reba barked at Tom.
"Why don't you get up and let 'em both sit down!" was Tom's reply.

☆ ☆ ☆ ☆ ☆

A wife has been defined as the mate who is forever complaining about not having a thing to wear at the very same time that she complains about having no room in the closet.

☆ ☆ ☆ ☆ ☆

Eddie Bronfman says that with today's hair styles for women, some awful short and others gussied-up all over the place, it is a little hard to tell whether she has been to a beauty salon or to the taxidermist.

☆ ☆ ☆ ☆ ☆

I've sometimes thought of marrying, and then I've thought again.
Noel Coward, 1956

A cynic once said, "Before marriage, a man yearns for the woman he loves. After marriage, the 'Y' becomes silent."

It is said that a man advertised to sell a complete set of the Encyclopedia Britannica. When asked by a prospective buyer why he was selling it, he said, "I don't need it any more. My wife knows everything."

And now a few humorous tales about the mother-in-law, a dominant part of family life and the source, however unfair, of many humorous stories.

Where are the father-in-law stories? Nobody seems to know, but the lack of them seems to indicate just where the real, actual power rests in resolving family problems.

☆ ☆ ☆ ☆ ☆

"Teddy," his wife said, looking up from the daily newspaper, "it says here that our government is going to cut overhead. They are going to eliminate eight overage destroyers."

"Sorry to hear that, Dear. I'm sure you'll miss your mother very much."

☆ ☆ ☆ ☆ ☆

"Incidentally," Teddy continued, "your mother called just before you got home."

"Good. And how is she?"

"Fair to meddling, as usual."

☆ ☆ ☆ ☆ ☆

For many husbands, the "blessed event" occurs when mother-in-law goes home.

☆ ☆ ☆ ☆ ☆

A man, Ben Fliegle, went to a bookstore and asked to see a book titled, *"How to Control Your Mother-in-Law."*

"Our fiction department is in the rear, left side," grinned the salesman.

Alex announced that he was leaving his wife because of another woman...his mother-in-law.

☆ ☆ ☆ ☆ ☆

For twenty-five years, my mother-in-law and I were perfectly contented and happy. Then we met.

☆ ☆ ☆ ☆ ☆

"We're having definitions of words, Dad, and the teacher asked some tough ones."

"Interesting," his father replied. "What kind of questions do they ask? Give me an example."

"Monologue was one. Define monologue."

"That one I know," his father responded, "it's a conversation between your Grandma and me."

☆ ☆ ☆ ☆ ☆

"It's just not true, George," his mother-in-law said, shaking her head, "it's simply not so. I have never, never made a fool out of you. I have always given you every opportunity to develop your own natural talent in that regard."

" SOMEONE WOULD LIKE TO LISTEN TO YOU."

The mother-in-law had listened to a spat that had gone on for over an hour and she was fed up with it. "You married Susie for better or worse," she yelled at her son-in-law as he started for the door.

"I sure did," the fellow shot back, "but that was five years ago. So when is it going to get better?"

☆ ☆ ☆ ☆ ☆

Tim Souther was telling the boys at the office about his constant bickering with his mother-in-law. "Just the other day, she told me she was going to dance on my grave," Tim told them. "So, you know what? I've decided to be buried at sea."

☆ ☆ ☆ ☆ ☆

An Indiana fellow complains that his mother-in-law has an untreatable speech impediment...she won't stop talking.

☆ ☆ ☆ ☆ ☆

Then there was the batty mother-in-law who went on the pill because she didn't want any more grandkids.

☆ ☆ ☆ ☆ ☆

What a superb pleasure trip I just had! I drove my mother-in-law to the airport.

☆ ☆ ☆ ☆ ☆

When our family doctor is unable to cure terrible cases of hiccups suffered by one of his patients, he sends the patient to our house to take a look at my mother-in-law. Shock works almost every time.

☆ ☆ ☆ ☆ ☆

Talk about unmitigated gall. When my mother-in-law came to live with us, I greeted her with, "Mother, my house is your house." It made me feel good to say it and I thought she'd really appreciate it. But it was a mistake. A year later, she sold the house.

☆ ☆ ☆ ☆ ☆

He'd love to go out and drown his troubles but he can't get his mother-in-law in the water.

Sandy Tewfig was taking his mother-in-law to the doctor in a nearby town when he was stopped by a highway policeman. "We just got a call that someone in your family had fallen out."

"Thank goodness," the son-in-law said. "I thought I'd gone stone deaf!"

☆ ☆ ☆ ☆ ☆

The Judge asked Bob Spiegel if he was sure that it was his mother-in-law who was driving the car that had hit him.

"Of course. I swear it. Why, there's no mistaking her laugh."

☆ ☆ ☆ ☆ ☆

It is amazing at how small a price may the wedding ring be placed upon a worthless hand; but, by the beauty of our law, what heaps of gold are indispensable to take it off!

Douglas Jerrold - 1858

☆ ☆ ☆ ☆ ☆

One day, a bum came to the back door of Tom Pettigrew and his mother-in-law answered the knock.

"Ma'am, I could sure use some old beer bottles to sell...to raise a little cash. Could you help me out?"

"Do I look like the sort who drinks beer!" she yelled.

"Well, then, any old vinegar bottles on hand?" the tramp inquired.

☆ ☆ ☆ ☆ ☆

Mike Kienzler claims that his big-mouth mother-in-law was in a restaurant and ordered soup. But when she began to eat it, four couples stood and began to dance.

☆ ☆ ☆ ☆ ☆

Otto Kerber was about half drunk in the neighborhood bar and the bartender could see he was feeling bad. "What's the trouble, Otto? What's bothering you?"

"I had an awful blowout with my mother-in-law," Otto replied. "She was so mad, she said she wouldn't speak to me for a week."

"Heck, Otto," the bartender said, "you oughta be out celebrating!"

"Maybe I would be," Otto said, "if today wasn't the end, the last day of that week."

Could it be that mothers weep at their daughter's marriage because of the tendency of girls to marry men like their fathers?

☆ ☆ ☆ ☆ ☆

Peter Gerber says that last month his mother-in-law visited the local zoo and had to buy two tickets...one to get in and the other to get out again.

☆ ☆ ☆ ☆ ☆

Jack Johnson's mother-in-law never got back from her shopping trip. Terribly worried, the Johnsons didn't know what to do. But the next day, in the mail, there came a letter, "Send $5,000 at once or we'll send her back!"

☆ ☆ ☆ ☆ ☆

It is difficult to know when stories about mothers-in-law are true or just...stories. Consider the story about the mother-in-law who forgot to put out the garbage one wintery morning but, when she saw the garbage truck arrive, she ran out to follow it down the alley, holding her sack of garbage. "Am I too late?" she yelled.
"Nope," they called back. "Jump in."

☆ ☆ ☆ ☆ ☆

There's no excuse for a husband not to know what's wrong with him. It's just that he hasn't been listening to his mother-in-law.

☆ ☆ ☆ ☆ ☆

Although up in years, Sam's mother-in-law was determined to learn how to drive. On her very first time behind the wheel, she moaned, "Sam, I don't know what to do!"
Sam sighed, blew his nose and said, "Just imagine I'm doing the driving."

☆ ☆ ☆ ☆ ☆

Sam and Maybelle were having a terrible argument. Finally, his wife shouted, "I wish I'd taken my mother's advice and never married you."
"Are you saying that your mother tried to convince you not to marry me?"
"That's exactly what I mean," Sam's wife snapped.
"My God!" whispered Sam, "I've misjudged that good woman!"

☆ ☆ ☆ ☆ ☆

I dislike saying it, but my mother-in-law is so fat she can open the front door without ever leaving the kitchen.

"I KNEW YOU'D LIKE IT."

My mother-in-law is wonderful at saving. She makes her own yogurt simply by placing a pint of milk on a shelf, then staring at it for five minutes.

☆ ☆ ☆ ☆ ☆

Abe Gordon tells us that his mother-in-law has a speech impediment. It seems that every minute or so, she pauses to breathe. He says his mother-in-law isn't really so ugly...it is just that she has this awful birthmark between her ears.

☆ ☆ ☆ ☆ ☆

Pete Foster's mother-in-law was a marvelous singer with a truly amazing voice. What do we mean by amazing? Well, she was practicing the other day and two factories shut down for lunch.

☆ ☆ ☆ ☆ ☆

Elmer Jordan's mother-in-law boasts that she started with nothing and is a self-made woman. Elmer said that he was glad to know the Lord was relieved of the blame.

A lady one day spoke to Jerrold about the beauty of an infant. In her enthusiasm, she said, "Really, I cannot find words to convey to you even a faint idea of its pretty ways."

"I see," said Jerrold. "It's a child more easily conceived than described."

Douglas Jerrold - 1858

☆ ☆ ☆ ☆ ☆

Talk about overweight! My mother-in-law is so fat that the other day, when she began to skip rope, the police came and stopped her because it registered 8 on the Richter scale.

☆ ☆ ☆ ☆ ☆

When Cliff Wanamaker got home after a night out on the town, his mother-in-law met him at the door. Drunken Cliff stepped back, then yelled, "You, Madam, are the ugliest female I've ever seen."

Not to be outdone, she yelled back, "And you're the very drunkest man I've ever seen."

"That could be," Cliff said slowly, "but tomorrow, I'll be sober."

☆ ☆ ☆ ☆ ☆

"My mother-in-law is a remarkable woman," Sam Snyder said. "She is eighty-five years old and never uses glasses...just drinks straight out of the bottle."

☆ ☆ ☆ ☆ ☆

A man in love is incomplete until he is married. Then he is finished.

Zsa Zsa Gabor

☆ ☆ ☆ ☆ ☆

Marriage was all a woman's idea and for man's acceptance of the pretty yoke, it becomes us to be grateful.

Phyllis McGinley

☆ ☆ ☆ ☆ ☆

Women are one of the Almighty's enigmas to prove to men that He knows more than they do.

Ellen Glasglow

Love matches, so called, have illusion for their father and need for their mother.

Neitzche

☆ ☆ ☆ ☆ ☆

Love matches are made by people who are content, for a month of honey, to condemn themselves to a life of vinegar.

Countess of Blessington

☆ ☆ ☆ ☆ ☆

A good marriage would be between a blind wife and a deaf husband.

Montaigne

☆ ☆ ☆ ☆ ☆

In olden times, the report has it that sacrifices were made at the altar. Well, they haven't changed at all!

☆ ☆ ☆ ☆ ☆

Mothers-in-law take it on the chin when it comes to jokes about the family. Consider this variant on a joke once told by Abraham Lincoln.

It seems that Eddie Busher's mother-in-law needed work so very much that she hired out to a farmer as a scarecrow in his cornfield. She did so well at it that she got a bonus not only for keeping the crows away, but they brought back the corn they had stolen the year before!

☆ ☆ ☆ ☆ ☆

Pete Vasconselles's mother-in-law was so dadblamed bossy that he quit calling her "Mother" and simply said, "Hey, Sir."

☆ ☆ ☆ ☆ ☆

Tom Jacoby claims that his mother-in-law is such a rotten cook that her garbage can has an ulcer.

☆ ☆ ☆ ☆ ☆

Talk about a big mouth...my wife's mother has the champion of them all. Why, that woman's mouth is so big, she can eat a banana sideways!

"AND FOR OUR WOODEN ANNIVERSARY HE GAVE ME A TOOTHPICK"

Even my doctor recognizes my mother-in-law for what she really is. When we took her to see the doc, he told us, "I can't help her. Take her to a veterinarian."

☆ ☆ ☆ ☆ ☆

"You surprised me, Susie, when you allowed your daughter to marry Dick Stout. I thought you couldn't stand him."

"I can't," Susie replied, her jaw set determinedly. "But I just wanted him where I could be his mother-in-law for a time."

☆ ☆ ☆ ☆ ☆

She told her son-in-law that her daughter is a woman who loves the simple things in life, which explains why she married him.

☆ ☆ ☆ ☆ ☆

There is one distinctive quality about my mother-in-law. She is so fat that she's taller lying down than standing!

As I was walking in the park, I saw an elderly man on a park bench and he was weeping pitifully. I felt so bad about him that I walked up, put my hand on his shoulder and said, "Oh, Sir, it can't be that bad. Would you like to tell me about your trouble? Would it make you feel better?"

"Thank you, Mister," the old boy said. "But I got to thinking about an experience I had some twenty-five years past. I went to my lawyer to tell him I was going to shoot my mother-in-law. He talked me out of it, telling me that I'd spend 30 years in jail if I went through with it. And that's why I'm crying. If I hadn't listened to that jerk, I'd be a free man today!"

The British had an organization that Americans are now considering adopting. It seems that in England, they had a men's club, Bachelors' Anonymous. The club provided a unique way to treat the problem of bachelors wanting to marry. They send over a mother-in-law in nightgown, hair curlers and a mud pack.

☆ ☆ ☆ ☆ ☆

Cliff described his wife's mother as having a figure like one million dollars...all in loose change.

☆ ☆ ☆ ☆ ☆

George Strickland describes his mother-in-law in this way: "She's got a head so inexcusably ugly that she spends three hours at the beauty parlor just to get an estimate. And if she accepts the price they give her, the boss adds a million dollars to their liability policy. They say that in the neighborhood where she lives, when people have uncontrollable hiccups, they take that person over for a look at her and the cure is miraculously immediate."

☆ ☆ ☆ ☆ ☆

They say that when his wife's father carried his own bride over the threshold, she was so darned big that her dad had to make three trips!

☆ ☆ ☆ ☆ ☆

Tom Appleby never says much about his mother-in-law. We always thought that they got along remarkably well...until Tom declared that if she lived in India, she'd be sacred.

Roger Grauman was painting the house when the ladder gave way and he fell to the ground. He recovered and immediately went to his lawyer, saying, "I want to file charges against my mother-in-law, to sue her good for pulling that ladder out from under me when I was painting my house."

"But are you quite sure it was she who did it?"

"Absolutely. I'd recognize that laugh anywhere!"

☆ ☆ ☆ ☆ ☆

When Tom lost his mother-in-law, he was approached by a friend who offered condolences, "Tom, it sure must be hard to lose a mother-in-law like your superlative one."

"Hard," Tom replied, "it's danged near impossible."

☆ ☆ ☆ ☆ ☆

"And how was your physical exam?" Adolph asked his mother-in-law.

"Went just fine," she replied. "The doctor surprised me when he said that my breasts were like a sixteen-year-old's."

"Yeah? And what'd he have to say about your big, fat ass?"

"He never so much as mentioned you."

☆ ☆ ☆ ☆ ☆

There was a Sunday in May when Tom was out on the golf course with a friend. They had reached the sixth hole when a funeral procession passed by. Tom took of his cap, bowed his head and stood as if in prayer.

"That was might nice of you, Tom," his good buddy said.

"Well, I got to tell you...she wasn't a bad mother-in-law at all."

☆ ☆ ☆ ☆ ☆

Johnny Jenkins realized for the first time that his mother-in-law's opinion of him didn't amount to a hill of beans. She gave him a gift labeled HERS and ITS.

☆ ☆ ☆ ☆ ☆

My wife claims her mother is a superb cook but I know otherwise. I learned a short time back, that she sold her stew to South American Indians who use it to poison their arrows.

☆ ☆ ☆ ☆ ☆

There's one exception to the rule that "absence makes the heart grow fonder." Yep! That's right. That exception is my mother-in-law.

125

"MARGE, I HAVEN'T SEEN YOUR FACE SINCE THE EPA
DECLARED PASSIVE SMOKE A CARCINOGEN."

"Why so down-in-the-mouth, Joe?" his friend asked.

"Well, it's my mother-in-law. Last week we had a terrible argument and now she's trying to influence my wife against me."

"What was the argument about, Joe?"

"Well, I merely pointed out that she should straighten her stockings, that they were wrinkled."

"Well, that doesn't seem so bad."

"But she wasn't wearing any."

☆ ☆ ☆ ☆ ☆

Tom Patton applied for a job as security guard at a nearby factory.

The employment manager looked him over and shook his head. "Mister, I don't think you qualify because we need a forceful, tough, fearless and suspicious person who is big and tough and not afraid of physical violence. You don't seem built for the job."

"Oh, don't worry about that," Tom replied. "It's my mother-in-law who wants the job!"

We were all delighted to hear that George Townsend had developed a new attachment for his mother-in-law. We were all encouraged to hear about it. Gave us new hope concerning our own...until we heard him say that the attachment we'd heard about fit perfectly...over her mouth!

☆ ☆ ☆ ☆ ☆

The fellow lay on the psychiatrist's couch and began to tell the doctor of his problem.

"I simply can't get it out of my mind," he began. "There I am, brandishing two enormous rattlesnakes as she runs hot on my heels. It scares me to death. Those fierce eyes, the long, sharp fangs, the scaly skin and that terrible, foul-smelling breath."

"It does sound unbearable," the doctor agreed.

"You haven't heard anything, yet," the patient said. "Wait till I tell you about the snakes."

☆ ☆ ☆ ☆ ☆

They have it all worked out among certain tribes in Africa. When they have a wedding reception, the thing they all look forward to is a toasted mother-in-law.

☆ ☆ ☆ ☆ ☆

When Junie Cerf returned from a week-long business trip, he observed, to his deep disgust, that his mother-in-law had come for a visit. He knew she was there because he saw her broomstick hanging on the closet door.

☆ ☆ ☆ ☆ ☆

Shrew: A woman who destroys her son-in-law's peace of mind by giving him a piece of hers.

☆ ☆ ☆ ☆ ☆

There's an old, old story still told out in the Ozark Mountains about a sad incident that occurred about 1930. It seems that a farmer's mule went on a rampage and kicked the farmer's mother-in-law to death. A huge crowd came for the funeral, mostly men. The preacher commented, "This old lady sure must have been mighty well thought of, in these parts, to have so many men quit work to come to her funeral."

"They ain't here for the funeral," the bereaved farmer said. "They came here to buy the mule."

Freddy Barthomew came into the bar and reported that he had just bought his mother-in-law a new chair. Now that pleased us all very much until he mentioned that as soon as he got home he would plug it in.

They say that in the more formal parts of England, it is the custom for husbands to stand a respectful distance away when addressing their mothers-in-law. There is a measure of respect. In American, it is a matter of safety.

Most husbands are willing to split the blame for their divorce. Half of it to the wife and half of it to the mother-in-law.

☆ ☆ ☆ ☆ ☆

Of course, one must expect a light bulb joke with mothers-in-law to do the turning. So how many of them does it take to change a light bulb? A hundred...one to change it, the other ninety-nine to say, "I told you so!"

☆ ☆ ☆ ☆ ☆

The courts have been accused of unjust and excessive punishment for bigamy. Aren't two mothers-in-law punishment enough?

☆ ☆ ☆ ☆ ☆

The tale goes that Eddie Rickenbach's father-in-law died without saying any last words of advice for his children. It seems that his wife was with him to the very end.

☆ ☆ ☆ ☆ ☆

Generally speaking, mothers-in-law are generally speaking.

☆ ☆ ☆ ☆ ☆

An elderly woman ran up the stairs to the church, late for the wedding. An usher asked to see her invitation.
"I don't have one," she said.
"Well, then, are you a friend of the groom?"
"I should say not," snapped the woman, "I'm the bride's mother."

George's mother-in-law needed a new set of false teeth, so he escorted her to the dentist. "I don't understand why you need a new set," the dentist said. "I made you a new set not over six months ago."

"Don't be concerned, Doctor. This is her tenth set. She wears 'em out."

☆ ☆ ☆ ☆ ☆

Bob Evan's mother-in-law talks so much that he actually gets hoarse listening to her.

"THAT WAS A DELICIOUS DINNER MILDRED!
NOW, WHAT DID YOU DO TO THE CAR?"

3

HUSBANDS and WIVES
Sometimes They Both Win

Cliff and Sandra Hathaway were lunching at a lovely beach hotel in San Diego. Sandra choked on a clump of sand in the salad. Cliff loudly called the waiter over and complained, "Waiter, there's sand in our salad!"

The waiter replied, "Sir, did you come here to enjoy the beach or to complain about it?"

"Waiter," Cliff replied, "we came here to enjoy the beach, not to eat it."

An example of contemporary progress is the fact that today's housewife has gone from dishpan hands to push-button fingers.

After examining his grandson Charlie's grades, Grampa said, "Charlie, I just don't understand it. How is it that you come home with these absolutely disgraceful grades?"

"The only way I can explain it, Gramps, is heredity!"

Jane and Elvira were old classmates. They met downtown one day and decided to have a cup of coffee and discuss their lives. "And how is your husband?" Jane asked Elvira. "All right, I guess," Elvira answered. "I don't think he loves me anymore."

Jane was shocked. "Really! How could that be? Are you sure?"

"Pretty darn sure," Elvira replied. "He hasn't been home for over a year."

It's a lot harder to be a mother today than it was, say, fifty years ago when most families had only one car. Now most families have two cars and mother has to wait until **both** get home.

A modern home is one where a mere switch controls everything but the kids.

Elmer Rankin can remember back when marriages produced more triangles on the clothesline than in the courtroom.

Ebenezer Meyer was a cantankerous old guy whose daughter seemed quite serious about a young man. Ebenezer told her he wanted to meet the guy. The suitor came to the house and Ebenezer asked, "As I get it, you want to become my son-in-law. That right?"

"Not at all, Sir," the young man said, "but I see no way to avoid it if I marry your daughter."

The old adage that "marriages are made in heaven" doesn't tell it all...because thunder and lightning are made there, too.

Susie: "I got a new insight into marriage while I was at church last Sunday."
Maisie: "Yeah? Tell me about it."
Susie: "Well, like everyone else, I always thought that a single marriage, you know, monogamy, was the way to go. But not now."
Maisie: "Wow! That is a shift for you. What did the preacher say?"
Susie: "I heard him say distinctly, 'four better, four worse, four richer, four poorer.' That makes sixteen."

The last seven years of married life had not been easy on Tom Lesser. His wife, Sylvia, had grown more and more domineering even to the point of Tom insisting that she see a psychiatrist. After much pleading, Sylvia finally agreed to go, much to Tom's surprise. After coming out of the office, following an hour with the psychiatrist, Tom asked, "How did it go, Dear? Helpful?"

"I'm not sure," Sylvia replied. "It took most of the hour to convince him that the couch would look a whole lot better on the right instead of the left side of the door."

An accusation I always hated,
Is "You're a couch potato!"
That it was false, I never doubted,
Until the day I noticed I'd sprouted.

♥ ☆ ♥ ☆ ♥

Today we are discovering a mathematical truth: The home circle can't be kept square with a triangle.

♥ ☆ ♥ ☆ ♥

The Museum of Modern Art was their first stop. And they thoroughly enjoyed the novelty of the visit, until they stood in front of a huge, very abstract painting. They stared at it for a few moments, then Adolph turned to Sarah and whispered, "Let's get out of here before they accuse us of messing up that painting."

"DO YOU PROMISE TO LOVE, CHERISH, AND PROTECT HER IN SICKNESS AND IN HEALTH AND UNTIL MEDICARE CAN TAKE OVER?"

Pop and Mom were very disappointed in the grades that their son brought home. "The only consolation I can find in these awful grades," his father said, "is that I know he wasn't cheating."

The law is too often distorted in the courtrooms of today. Consider the couple who had their marriage annulled and sued the minister who married them...for malpractice!

It was a mid-July day in Peoria, Illinois, and Johnny's mother had invited several of her friends over for dinner. Just before time to eat, she took Johnny aside and told him to say the blessing. "But what'll I say, Mom?"
"Before we eat, you say what you've heard me say many times."
The boy stood with the other folks around the table and when his mother nodded to him, he said, "Good Lord...Oh Good Lord...why did I invite these people on a hot day like this?"

Love: a more-or-less temporary insanity curable by marriage (more or less).

It was his first car and cost almost nothing. And he got what he paid for...a car dented on every inch of its surface, obviously a carrier in many, many collisions. But the boy was mighty proud of this, his first car, and was busy washing it down when his father walked up, observed the car, the boy, the washing, then said, "Son, when you get done washing your car, I think you ought to also iron it."

Mrs. Cedric Gotbux was a New York dowager. She was snobbish, haughty and always a bore! One evening, for dinner, her cook served her ox tongue. The dowager couldn't identify the meat at first, so called in the cook. "What is this?"
"Ox tongue, Ma'am," the cook answered.
"Ox tongue!" the dowager snapped. "How dare you serve me something out of a cow's mouth!"
"Well, Ma'am, this morning you ate eggs."

A good husband is one who checks his pockets every time he passes a mailbox.

Dr. and Mrs. Jacob Gover were given a very hard time by I.R.S. agents over their income tax returns. The good doctor, a proctologist, was fed up. Suddenly the revenue agent asked, "Pardon me, Doctor, but I'm not sure I understand just what a proctologist does. Could you explain it to me?"

"Certainly," said the doctor. "A proctologist is a brain surgeon for I.R.S. agents."

Here are some puns from that great pun-fun-bunch, *"The Pun American Newsletter,"* headquartered at 1165 Elmwood Place, Deerfield, IL 60015.

In Toronto, Canada, the Infant Feeding Action Coalition promoted breast-feeding by distributing posters. One poster read: "Sometimes it's OK to suck up to the boss."

Another advertises: "Fast food outlets -- two locations."

Another pun went something like this: Bob Classen was a bus driver who saw his wife come onto the bus and then said, "Your fare, Dear."

His wife replied, "That's for sure, Honey!"

There was a headline in a Bakersfield, CA newspaper that read, "Husband eyes wife's seat on City Council."

♥ ☆ ♥ ☆ ♥

When Jasper Gunov was courting his wife, Jennifer, he walked up to her at the local dance. Jasper, who owned an auto repair shop, asked, "May I have the next dents, Dear?"

♥ ☆ ♥ ☆ ♥

Then there was the Unitarian boy who married an Amish girl. He drove her buggy. (Reported by Emily Meter, Deerfield, IL).

Mary Boyer was no prude but it was just a bit too much when she and her husband walked into a dry cleaners and noticed the sign, "Drop your pants here for best results."

Or consider these hit titles of potential western songs, as conceived by Scott Summers of Harvard, IL:

He Used to Go Bananas for Me -- Now I've Lost Appeal.
Love Ain't Nothing But a Tennis Score.
If You're Burning With Desire, Then I'm Your Match.
Take Your Cheatin' Heart and Beat It.
We Used to be Drinkin' Buddies -- Now All She Does Is Whine.
Why Did I Go Ape for that Baboon.
We Used to Be Lovebirds -- Now I'm Eating Crow.
You're a Zero for Trying to Score with Me.

Two old friends were discussing their daughters and how hard it was to properly raise girls today." Mamie, how old is your daughter?" Sarah asked.

"She's sixteen," Mamie replied. "And yours, Sarah?"

"Mine's at that difficult age when her voice is changing from 'no' to 'yes'"

A successful man is one who makes more money than his wife can spend. A successful woman is one who can find such a man.

Lana Turner

Sarah Jane was showing her father a photograph of her finance, whom father had yet to meet. "I can't wait to have you meet him, Daddy," Sarah gushed. "He's a true outdoorsman. That photo of us walking through the cow pasture on his uncle's farm shows what kind of he-man he is!"

"I'm not so sure, Sarah Jane. Anybody with outdoors-sense knows that you don't walk through a cow pasture with your head up looking at the sky!"

"Your husband's last words were, 'I'm not going to dim my lights until he dims his!' "

Mr. and Mrs. Robert Petefish had given up their home and taken a nice little apartment in a retirement home. One night the phone rang and Mrs. Petefish answered it. "Do you have a Sexauer there?" a voice asked.

"Certainly not!" Mrs. Petefish replied. "Anymore, we don't even have a coffee break."

Indiana humorist George Ade once said that a little incompatibility is the spice of life, particularly if he has income and she is patable.

Mary and Peter Justice were up in years but attending a party of much younger people. One of them asked Peter how he and Mary were feeling, and Peter responded: "Let me put it this way, young man, Mary always serves dessert first!"

A young woman, two months pregnat, went to see her over-worked physician, the only doctor in a town of 50,000. He was in a hurry to leave on an emergency call, so he asked her to quickly bare her stomach, then reached in his desk and took out a rubber stamp, which he pressed beside her navel. Then he said good-by and rushed off.

At home, she and her husband tried to read the words printed on her belly, but they were too small. Even with a magnifying glass, the words were illegible. So they found a magnifying glass that would magnify a hundred times and tried to read it with that. It worked. The stamp read: "When your husband can read this without his glasses, it's time to get yourself to the hospital."

The Rabbi arrived at the gate to heaven only to find the attendants in disarray, running hither and yon and totally distraught. "What's the matter?" the Rabbi asked.

"It's Adam and Eve," an angel told him. "We can't find them. We've looked everywhere. Where can they be?"

"I'll bet I can find them," the Rabbi said.

"Be our guest," the angel replied delightedly. "Come in, make yourself at home and we'll give you a pair of spare wings if you locate 'em."

In a short time, the Rabbi returned with Adam and Eve in tow. "Tell us," the angels demanded. "Oh, Rabbi, tell us true -- how did you locate them?"

"Easy as pie," the Rabbi said. "I just looked for a gal and a guy without navels."

One of the safest ways to assure a continuing, happy marriage is to be sure the wife is a treasure and the husband a treasury.

♥ ☆ ♥ ☆ ♥

The telephone rang and Gretchen got up to answer it. "Mrs. Stern," the voice greeted her, "this is Doctor Daniel Dove and I want to report on your husband's physical examination. I've got good news and bad!"

"Oh, Doctor, please give me the good news first."

"Very well. Your husband, Sam, has only thirty-six hours to live."

"Oh, my God, Doctor. What could be worse than that?"

"I've been trying to reach you for an entire day."

The girl who remembers her first kiss now has a daughter who can't recall her first husband.

The St. Louis woman was telling the doctor all about her troubles. "It's my poor husband, Doctor. All he does all day is sit around and blow smoke rings."

"Not to worry, Ma'am," the doctor told her. "Lots of smokers do that."

"But, Doctor, my husband doesn't smoke."

Theresa Dobbins was a wonderful woman, superb housewife, good mother, even though she had not gone to school past the fourth grade. One day, she received a phone call asking for her daughter, Jennifer. "She's done gone off to her class," Theresa replied.

"Which class is that?" the caller asked.

"I think they calls it domestic silence," Theresa replied.

Marriage, formerly considered a contract, is now more akin to a 90-day option.

ENGAGEMENT RING -- Matrimony's promissory note.

"Tell me, Rachel," her friend asked, "how's your boy, Robert, doin' in college?"

"Just fine," was the reply. "He's taking something called chemistry and he wrote us that the other day in class, he had to take two gallons of hydrogen and a gallon of oxygen and made water."

"Well, I should think he would, Rachel!" her friend replied.

A traveling salesman named Cox,
Got hitched on one of his stops,
To a widow named Kidd,
Who then flipped her lid,
When she saw there were three little cocks.

"Eddie and Susie are sure a well-mated couple, aren't they!"

"You bet they are! Eddie snores like a thunderstorm and his wife is stone deaf."

♥ ☆ ♥ ☆ ♥

"They say," Eddie Jones remarked, "that the accelerated and continuing divorce rate indicates that the good old U.S.A. is still the Land of the Free."

"In the same vein of thought," his friend remarked, "the marriage rate also demonstrates that we remain the Home of the Brave!"

♥ ☆ ♥ ☆ ♥

Woman's tears: The strongest and most effective water power.

♥ ☆ ♥ ☆ ♥

"Hey, Buddy, I hear you got married," Joe Thoma's friend said. "I guess you're now the captain on the good ship matrimony, eh?"

"Nope. My wife's the captain. I'm the second mate. She was married before."

♥ ☆ ♥ ☆ ♥

"Mary, there is a report from Jerusalem that they've discovered an ancient castle with all the furniture, drapes, utensils in perfect condition...after three thousand years of burial. Isn't that amazing?"

"Not so much as you think, George, haven't I always told you it pays to buy good furniture?"

♥ ☆ ♥ ☆ ♥

It's not fair to visit all
The blame on Eve for Adam's fall;
The most Eve did was to display
Contributory negligence.

Oliver Herford

♥ ☆ ♥ ☆ ♥

Art is the fourth guy she's led to the **halter**.

♥ ☆ ♥ ☆ ♥

Bachelor: Half a pair of scissors.

Edna Reilly remarked to husband Bill that their grandchildren sure brightened up the home when they came to visit.

"They sure do," Bill agreed. "They never turn off the lights."

Two guys who had not seen one another in several years met on the street. "Glad to see you again," one said, "but you don't look well. You've aged more than somewhat."

"It's because I'm trying to keep young," the other replied.

"Really? But I don't understand. Trying to keep young?"

"Yep! Nine of them."

"We have a terrible time making it on Eddie's income." his wife told her best friend. "How do you manage?"

"We get along OK," her friend said. "You see, we work on our budget every evening. That saves us lots of money."

"Really? I don't understand."

"Well, by the time we get it balanced, it's too darned late to go anywhere."

" Marriage is a blessed relationship; a union in which each partner gives mutual devotion and respect to the other. Now let's all have a good laugh and get down to business."

Home has been defined as a sanctuary from which, on a clear day, you can see the finance company.

A cute girl answered a advertisement for a nurse to take care of a newborn child. She had all the necessary credentials and the wife nodded approval. "But," she said to the applicant, "Are you decent, faithful, kind and considerate and of a loving disposition? are you also...?"

"Madam," the girl interrupted, "are you wanting me to take care of your baby or your husband?"

A home has been defined as a residence with wall-to-wall carpeting, wall-to-wall windows and back-to-the-wall financing.

"Many a man that cud rule a hundherd millyon sthrangers with an ir'n hand is careful to take off his shoes in the' front hallway whin he comes home late at night."
Finley Peter Dunne, <u>Mr. Dooley on Making a Will</u>, 1919.

Wedlock: The deep, deep peace of the double bed after the hurly-burly of the chaise-lounge.
Mrs. Patrick Campbell

Mary Jo complained to her friend, Leah, that she had an awful headache. "Too bad," Leah told her, "why don't you do as I do...get my husband to rub my forehead, then caress my back, then caress my neck, then massage my arms and give me a little kiss. Why don't you give it a try?"

"Great idea. When does your husband get home?"

There is one form of exercise that can sure change the life of people for the better and get them in the best of shape. And, that's that certain walk down the church aisle.

Politics doesn't make strange bedfellows -- marriage does.
Groucho Marx

"I have come to the conclusion never again to think of marrying, and for this reason: I can never be satisfied with anyone who would be blockhead enough to have me."
Abraham Lincoln in a letter to Mrs. O.H. Browning, April 1, 1838.

One way to live together and never have an argument is for both husband and wife to be hard-of-hearing and...to share the same hearing aid.

Jim Herrin was approaching sixty and had never thought much about aging. Then, one morning, he forgot his tie and left the breakfast table to get it, climbing up the stairs, down again and back to the table. "Sweetheart," he said to his wife. "Our friends may lie to us, our pride confuse us, our mirrors hide the truth, but that flight of stairs sure as heck tells me the truth about aging."

If you're stuck trying to open a bottle or can or the like, just tell a six-year-old not to touch it.

Child psychologists tell us not to upset our children when we correct them. But that makes it mighty difficult to reach the part of them that we need to work on to get them properly corrected.

"What an angel my husband is."
"Really? I thought him an incorrigible womanizer."
"True. But yesterday he went searching for gas leaks with a match."

It is true that, "fewer marriages would skid if more who said 'I do' did."

Lorin Barton described his son's wedding as "a dollar and sense affair."

His friend asked, "What's a dollar and sense affair?"

Lorin replied, "He hasn't a dollar, and she's shy of sense."

A baby can't hold very much by itself...but it can hold a marriage together.

A famous movie star was once asked by a reporter if she had ever been married. Her reply, "Occasionally."

That same lovely star was being discussed by two of her "friends." "They say that she's about to marry her 'x' husband," one gossip said.

"Really? I didn't know that," the other replied, "but isn't it odd that she lists them alphabetically!"

"I think the Willoughbys know something we don't."

The divorce rate is approaching 50%. From those figures, it would seem that a lot of couples who said, "I do...didn't."

Caleb and Lolita Houston made a mutual agreement to dispose of their bodies through cremation, not full-body burial. Lolita died first and, as agreed, Caleb had her cremated and placed her ashes in an urn that he kept on the mantelpiece.

Caleb liked to entertain and, after a decent interval had passed, began to have guests. After several months of entertaining with many of his guests flicking cigarette ashes in her urn, a friend came over one night, peered into the urn and remarked, "Say, Caleb, looks to me like the missus is puttin' on weight."

Every young girl should heed the warning that, as with a household pet, she should not respond to a whistle unless she can interpret it.

Isn't it strange that while banks frequently guarantee interest rates for several years, marriage licenses can't do the same?

Ike Funnel was a few bricks short of a full load, and when he came to town the boys had a great time with him. This one day, when Ike approached the guys at a party as they were all having a discussion over coffee, they asked, "Ike, do you know the name of this town?" "Nope," Ike replied. "Well, do you know the name of the county?" "No, don't believe I does." "Well, you surely heard of Jesus Christ?" Again, Ike replied, "No." At last they asked if he'd ever heard of God. "I think I have," Ike replied, "let...me...think.... Tell me, is his last name, Damn?"

Some of us remember the backwoods, hill county comedian, Bob Burns. He told the story of a friend who yanked his young son out of school because "the ig'erant principal was teaching the boy to spell 'taters' with a 'p'!"

In the little town of Elkhart, Illinois, there lived a poor but vigorous family named Petefish. Now, Elmer Petefish didn't work very hard or often, but he did produce a lot at home...they had a dozen kids.

One day, Elkhart's store, a general store, caught fire and the old fire engine of the village wouldn't start. So the townspeople got to work and did their best to put out the fire, but there simply were not enough of them and the fire raged, hotter and hotter.

Well, Elmer, isolated in his old house, didn't know what was going on in the village but he had to get some groceries so he loaded his family in his truck -- wife and twelve kids, and started down the hill for the village. He soon saw the fire as he coasted downhill toward it but he kept right on going and ended up with his truck in the middle of the burning store. "Get out, kids, and put out this fire!" he ordered. And they did. They took shirts, dresses, whatever they could get and managed to beat out the fire.

The townspeople thought them heroic enough to take up a collection and give the impoverished family a hundred dollars. "What's the first thing you're going to get with all that money, Elmer?" he was asked by the committee that brought him the gift.

Elmer thought about that a minute, then said, "Y'know, the first thing I'm gonna do is get those damn brakes on my truck fixed."

The man who marries for money will suffer for it...but in comfort!

"If worrying burned up calories, I'd be a size 5!"

Tom and Babe Sloan have so much fat
It makes them stand out in a crowd.
Without hesitation, I'd deem their foundations
The heaviest ever endowed.

Jonathan George brought his fiancee home to meet his parents. She was an enormous creature of almost 300 pounds! But the family had a pleasant evening with her. When Jonathan returned home, he asked his parents what they thought of her. "Well, Jonathan," his father said after a brief pause, "in the first place, there's a little too much of her." "And in the second place, too," his mother added.

This particular couple believed in moderation in all things. When they realized that they usually had sex several times a week, they decided to limit themselves and be moderate in that relationship, too. They vowed to have sex only during the months with an "R" in them. But they had forgotten that the months of May, June and July were without an "R".

Well, one evening, at supper, the man asked, "Dear, what month is this?"

"It's Augurst, Sweetheart," she replied.

"I'm returning this violin," she said to the proprietor of the music store. "We just can't use it."

"But, Madam, your family can get a lot of wonderful music out of this instrument."

"Maybe you think so," she replied, "but I suspect that somebody got it all out before I bought it!"

George and Mary Stokes were leaving church one Sunday morning when he saw a pocketbook in the bushes beside the walk. He grabbed it. "Holy smokes, Dear, it's chock full of money -- fives, tens, twenties."

"What'll we do with it, take it to the preacher?"

"Let me think about it a bit longer, Dear. I'm trying to decide if it's a temptation from the devil or the response to my prayer."

Edgar Snow was 82 years old when his wife finally talked him in to having a physical exam. So he went to the doctor's office and had a complete check-up. When he got home, she asked him how things turned out. "The doctor said I was OK, dear. He told me there was no reason at all why I couldn't live a normal full life...so long as I didn't try to enjoy it."

♥ ☆ ♥ ☆ ♥

Somebody defined monogamy as marriage that has only one wife...and hardly any lady friends.

♥ ☆ ♥ ☆ ♥

"Dear, I hate to tell you this, but we are so near dead-broke that if a burglar was to break in tonight and rob me, all he'd get would be practice."

147

"Howdy, Joe. And how's your wife?"
"Compared to what?"

John Rogers and his wife were enjoying a week's visit with their grandson. That is, they were until they discovered that the kid had put Crazy Glue in John's Preparation H.

As most Americans know, Abraham Lincoln was not only wise but very witty...and always to the point. One time he was asked why he never took a definite position in arguments between members of his Republican party. He responded that..."In a fight between man and wife, a third party should never get between the woman's skillet and the man's axe-handle."

"Daddy, before you married Mommy, who told you
how to drive?"

For a man to pretend to understand women is bad manners; for him to really understand them is bad morals.

Henry James

"How was the reception last night, Mary?"

"Very nice. Except that darned Agnes Smith. You know her? Agnes S. Smith?"

"Sure, I do. What about her?"

"I was so ashamed. She has no sense of decorum or the fitness of things. Why, she wore a black satin dress cut so low in back that you could see her initials."

Talk about snooty! That Mrs. Simkins is impossible. Why, she's so rich she sends her dishes to be dry-cleaned!

Any intelligent woman who reads the marriage contract, and then goes into it, deserves all the consequences.

Isadora Duncan

Edith and Paul Savage wanted tomatoes but they weren't priced. So she carried four of them to the check-out counter and asked the price. "They're a dollar apiece," the cashier said.

"What! A dollar apiece!" Paul shouted. "Why that's outrageous! Well, you can take them and you know what you can do with them, too."

"Sorry, I can't, Sir. There a $9.00 cucumber there already."

That Adam Sylvester is so crooked that when he pulls the wool over your eyes, it's 50% polyester.

♥ ☆ ♥ ☆ ♥

An elderly couple were sitting in the kitchen when the stove blew up and sent them both sailing out to land in a haystack.

"You OK, Paw?" the wife asked.

"Yep. Lucky, I guess. You OK, Ma?"

"Yep! Kinda enjoyed it. Seems like it's the first time we been out together in years."

Clarence Brown was preceded in death by his wife, Erma. Some ten years after she died, Clarence joined her in heaven and Erma was explaining how delightful it was. "Every night we have singing and dancing, then we play bingo and when you get tired of all that, you can go see an old Bing Crosby movie."

"Wonderful," Ernie said. "But it makes me derned mad to think that if it weren't for that oat bran I've been eating, I'd have been up here years ago."

Ike Blaise told his friend how he divided his income. "Forty percent goes for food. Thirty percent goes for the interest on our house and upkeep. Fifty percent is set aside for clothing and entertainment... ."

"But, Ike," his friend interrupted. "Already that makes 120%."

"I sure as hell know that."

A model husband has been described as one who is a working model with an adequate income.

A druggist posted this sign on the entry door: "Smoking, or forgetting your wife's birthday, can be hazardous to your health."

Seth Thomas was a New Hampshire newspaper columnist and a truly wise man. Once he wrote, "It is good when husband and wife have different mental traits. Some call it 'complementary stupidities,' meaning that the rocks in **her** head fit the holes in **his**."

A poker-playing buddy asked one of his friends home for supper. When they walked in the door, the surprised wife was really furious.

In a huff, she served them nothing but a cup of soup, a thin slice of turkey and a piece of bread.

Supper over (quickly), the husband said, "Hey, man, you'll have to have me over to your house for supper sometime soon, right?"

"Sure. How about tonight?"

There are lots of old-fashioned mothers who could and would like to tuck their kids in bed...but they can't stay awake that late!

Mary Jane was fifteen and certain that she had every right to do as she pleased with her room; yet she was very interested in world environmental problems. One day, her folks called Mary downstairs. "You called me, Mom an' Dad? What's up?"

"We want to talk about your room, Honey," Mother said.

"I thought so," Mary Jane replied. "It's my room and I'm old enough to do as I please in it."

"But it's in bad shape, Dear. I open the door and stuff falls out the door into the hall and the place smells bad."

"Well, what do you intend to do about it? I'm terribly busy studying the environment."

Pop stood up, shook his finger at Mary Jane and said, "You got two chances, little girl. You either get your room in first-rate shape by morning...or file an environmental impact statement."

"Good heavens, my wife! Has anybody seen my wife?!"

Their son was fourteen and a might difficult to handle. All this made it hard to decide on what to get him for his birthday. "Let's get him a bicycle," Mother said.

"I'm not sure," Papa said. "Do you think it'll make him behave better?"

"Not likely," Mother said. "But one thing sure...it'll spread it over a much wider area."

♥ ☆ ♥ ☆ ♥

Ed and Sue told their pastor that they never realized how much they had to be thankful for until they had to pay taxes on it all!

♥ ☆ ♥ ☆ ♥

Edith Rogers went to the undertakers to select a casket for her deceased husband.

"Here's a dandy, our end-of-the-month special," the undertaker suggested.

"Very nice. I'll take it," Edith said.

"A good selection. Now what kind of trimmins do you want on it?"

"I don't want any. That's what he died of."

"Your husband died of trimmins, Ma'am? I don't understand," the undertaker said.

"Well, he did," Edith replied. "Delirim trimmins."

♥ ☆ ♥ ☆ ♥

In the better areas of Chicago, the folks are so harassed by gunfire that they try to keep **down** with the Joneses.

♥ ☆ ♥ ☆ ♥

"Have you met Johnny's new wife yet?"

"Sure have. A bit overweight, I'd say."

"You can say that again. When I met her, she looked like she was poured into her dress and forgot to say 'when.'"

♥ ☆ ♥ ☆ ♥

Mary Simpkins was having her first dinner with Estee, the new daughter-in-law. When Mary complained of the coffee not being hot, Estee put her finger in the cup to test it.

"What a way to test coffee!" Mary said to her new daughter-in-law.

"Well, I could roll up my sleeve and test it with my elbow, but that takes more time," was the reply.

152

"When I got my hysterectomy, they removed the baby buggy but left me the play pen," said the mother of eight.

"What do you think of Cecilia Thomas? She sleeps with cats every night!"
"How awful. I wonder why."
"I suppose it's because she's married to Mr. Katz."

A bit of American wisdom was demonstrated at a medical school during a discussion of obstetrics. "Who is happier of two men, one with five million dollars or one with five kids?" asked the professor.
A student stood up to answer: "I'd guess the guy with five kids," he said.
"And why did you pick him?" the professor asked.
"Because the guy with all that money, five million bucks, isn't satisfied and wants more."

Alimony: Buying oats for a runaway horse. Or, a woman's cash surrender value.

There's an old story about the young farm couple who had just delivered their first child who only weighed two pounds. When the new father told his old dad about the kid weighing so little and all, the old man replied, "Well, son, looks to me like ya hardly got your seed back."

"Don't be surprised when I tell you that a seventy-six-year-old woman I know had a baby," announced the medical professor.
"But, Doctor," sang out one of the students, "that seems to be biologically impossible!"
"Well, depends on how you look at it. In this case the baby came fifty years ago when she was twenty-six."

♥ ☆ ♥ ☆ ♥

Jimmy and Rosie named their tenth child "Encore." Why? Because he wasn't on their program.

Some folks simply can never win. They are born losers. An example? There was a fellow who, when he put a seashell to his ear, always got a busy signal.

"You should have seen and heard my husband on our first date," Marie Wensler told her friend, Irma. "He was radiant, really. Why, it was love at first sight."

"I just can't believe it," Irma said. "A second look and he just might have changed his mind."

A contented family is one that practices the wisdom inherent in this saying: "One half of knowing what you want is knowing what you have to give up to get it."

A little town in southern Illinois had a sensational birth rate, and scientists decided to visit the place and find out the cause. So the sociologists, anthropologists, birth control specialists and other concerned scientists moved to the town prepared to do a six-month study of the causes of the town's high birth rate.

The day the research testing and all was to begin, the director of the million-dollar project stopped off at the single cafe in town and ordered coffee. When the waiter delivered his drink, the scientist detained him for a moment and asked, "Can you give me an idea as to why your town, above all others in this country, has such a high birth rate?"

The waiter thought a moment, then said, "I think I can. You see, every morning at 4:00, the C & A Railroad comes through town and blows its whistle at all three street crossings. That wakes up the folks here and, as you can guess, it's too damned late to go back to sleep and too damned early to get up."

Peter and Suzanne finally got married and lived happily ever after...for a few months.

Marriages may be made in heaven but it's certain that we humans are responsible for the maintenance work.

"Sir, don't you know it's terribly impolite to burp before my wife!"
"I'm sure sorry about that but I didn't know it was her turn."

Babies sure are lots of trouble
Avoiding them is double trouble.

A woman was in the hospital, having her first child. The distraught husband paced up and down the hospital hall until he could stand it no longer. He rushed to the desk and said, "I'm at my wit's end, Nurse. I've got to speak to her. Can you allow it?"

"Only for a moment," the nurse said. "Follow me."

The nurse left him beside his anguished, struggling wife who seemed in terrible agony. Her husband stared down at her, then said, "Dearest one, are you certain that you want to go through with this?"

A physician visited a California mental institution and asked a patient, "How did you get here? What was the nature of your illness?" He got this reply.

"It started when I got married and I guess I should never have done it. I got hitched to a widow with a grown daughter who then became my stepdaughter.

"My Daddy came to visit us, fell in love with my lovely stepdaughter, then married her. And so my stepdaughter was now my stepmother.

"Soon my wife had a son who was, of course, my daddy's brother-in-law since he is the half-brother of my stepdaughter, who is now, of course, my daddy's wife. So, as I told you, when stepdaughter married my daddy, she was at once my stepmother! Now, since my new son is brother to my stepmother, he also became my uncle.

"As you know, my wife is my step-grandmother since she is my stepmother's mother. (Don't forget that my stepmother is my stepdaughter). Remember, too, that I am my wife's grandson.

"But hold on just a few minutes more. You see, since I'm married to my step-grandmother, I am not only the wife's grandson and her hubby, but I am also my own grandfather.

"Now can you understand how I got put in this place?"

It's been said that "love" is a word of two vowels, two consonants and two fools.

A classic case of optimism occurred when Ellen Sankey asked her husband for enough money to buy a new baby bed.

"What's wrong with the old one?" Pete Sankey asked.

"We've had sixteen kids and every last one of 'em has used that bed. It's time for a new one because ours is unsteady."

"OK, OK," Pete said. "So buy one. But be sure you get one this time that's gonna last."

The average person's life consists of 20 years of their mother asking them where they're going; 40 years of having their spouse ask the same question; and in the end, the mourners wonder, too.

Evers and Ellis had not seen each other in many years. Now they had a long talk trying to fill in the gap of those years by telling about their lives. Finally, Evers invited Ellis to visit him in his new apartment. "I got a wife and three kids and I'd love to have you visit us."

"Great. Where do you live?"

"Here's the address. And there's plenty of parking behind the apartment. Park and come around to the front door, kick it open with your foot, go to the elevator and press the button with your left elbow, then enter! When you reach the sixth floor, go down the hall until you see my name on the door. Then press the doorbell with your right elbow and I'll let you in."

"Good. But tell me...what is all this business of kicking the front door open, then pressing elevator buttons with my right, then my left elbow?"

"Surely, you're not coming empty-handed."

The Ingalls should never have bought that water bed. Ever since owning one, they've been drifting apart.

Any mother understands Mary Stokes, the mother of six, when she says, "I live in a four bedlam house."

Frank Whitney passed on and went to heaven. Shortly afterwards, his devoted wife joined him and was surprised to see Frank and almost everyone else up there just working like crazy, shining the Pearly Gates, polishing stars, sweeping the heavens. There was nothing but work, work, work from morning until night. This disturbed her because having worked hard all her life, she thought heaven should be easier. So she asked for a couple of days off and visited down in Purgatory to see how things were there. To her surprise, people were sitting around doing absolutely nothing. After a couple of days of observing this, she asked the devil-attendant, "How come you people down here do nothing all day and we, up in heaven, work our fannies off?"

"That's easy," the devil-attendant said. "We get finished with our work quickly down here. Y'see, there's so many more of us!"

Their son was complaining about a portrait taken of Dad and Mom Jokisch, with Mom standing and Dad sitting. "I think that is typical of male chauvinism," the boy said. "Here you have mother standing and you, male and strong and quite able, sitting! Now that's not right, Dad! I'm ashamed of you."

"You don't understand, my boy," Elmer replied. "If you had asked us why positions were reversed, I'd have told you that just before we had that picture taken, I had just returned from a ten-mile hike and your mother had just finished her very first horseback ride. I couldn't stand and mother couldn't sit."

COURAGE -- Marrying a second time.

♥ ☆ ♥ ☆ ♥

Charlotte Simmons returned to the physician's office to receive a report on a general examination she had recently taken. The Doctor smiled and said, "Mrs. Simmons, I've got some good news for you."

Charlotte said, "Excuse me, Doctor, but it's **Miss** Simmons."

"Oh," the doctor said. "Well, if that's the case, I've got some bad news for you."

"DO YOU REALIZE IT'S ONLY 364 DAYS BEFORE IT ALL HAPPENS AGAIN?"

Helen Sloan was troubled with mice in her home. So she and her husband went to the pet shop and bought a cat. A week later, she took it back. "He's no good," she said. "And you told me he was good for mice."

"So, what's wrong, Ma'am?"

"This cat doesn't catch any mice, that's what's wrong. And you said he was good for mice."

"Well," the salesman said, "that's good for mice, isn't it?"

♥ ☆ ♥ ☆ ♥

There's an actress in Hollywood who destroyed so many homes that she's listed in the Yellow Pages as "Demolition Expert."

♥ ☆ ♥ ☆ ♥

Mary Simpson was almost crazy with her three kids. She complained to her best friend, "They're driving me nuts. Such pests, they give me no rest and I'm half-way to the nut hatch."

"What you need is a playpen to separate the kids from yourself," her friend said.

So Mary bought a playpen. A few days later, her friend called to ask how things were going.

"Superb! I can't believe it," Mary said. "I get in that pen with a good book and the kids don't bother me one bit!"

♥ ☆ ♥ ☆ ♥

Many a woman thinks that her husband is the world's greatest lover. The trouble is that she can never catch him at it.

♥ ☆ ♥ ☆ ♥

The little man came rushing into the minister's office, looking like he had lost his last friend. "Pastor, I'm desperate. I got a job that pays very little and every year, my wife presents me with another child. We got eleven. Each year brings me another. Pastor, please tell me what to do."

"My advice to you, Sir, is to do nothing. Simply lay off and do nothing, ab-so-lute-ly nothing, for a change."

♥ ☆ ♥ ☆ ♥

Bob and Irene Goodwin had been waiting at the restaurant for almost an hour for the fish they had ordered, when the waiter finally came to the table and announced that the fish would soon be ready. Bob asked, "Tell me, waiter, just what kind of bait are you using?"

WEDDING PRESENTS -- Society's trading stamps.

TALL TALES

Texas brags about big men, even big babies, but it is a well-known fact that in Sangamon County, Illinois, babies come in sizes they don't make clothing for! Yep! You want an example? All right! Consider this...A Sangamon County farm wife gave birth to a baby boy so big that he celebrated his birthday on July 4, 5 and 6.

Now that very baby, described above, has a father who is also notably tall. When he goes to put on his cap, he has to climb a chair to do it. Now that's tall.

There was a horrendous drought in Sangamon County, back in 1981. It ruined the corn crop, but one farm couple managed to get enough water to save their garden and produced enough food for the family for the winter. Here's how they did it. One night a very heavy fog rolled in and the resourceful farm wife simply sliced the fog in six-foot strips, then ran the strips through her wringer thus getting enough water to keep their garden watered. That's merely typical Illinois farm wife resourcefulness.

It may be thought that the author is prejudiced in favor of Illinois, but let him assure you that what he says here is the ironclad truth. Consider what he knows about the healthy climate in Illinois. In 1989, he drove his car from Springfield, Illinois to visit his wife who was visiting her family in Butte, Montana. When he got there, he was told that his wife was in the hospital and dying. When he reached the room, he found his dear helpmate gasping for breath. Well, he used good Illinois judgment, ran outside to where his car was parked, removed a tire, ran with it up to his wife's room, pressed down on the valve and all that good Illinois air flooded the room and went into his wife's lungs, and do you know, that she revived and was able to leave the hospital the next morning. Of course, he had to add air from a second tire to heal her that quickly.

Elmer Fudrucker had suffered with tinnitus for several years. Finally, his wife prevailed and made him see a physician, to help him stop the constant ringing in his ears. The doctor prescribed medicine, but Elmer returned it after a month's trial. "Doctor," he complained, "you know I've had this ringing in my ears for years now."

"Yes, I know," the Doctor said.

"Well, I had about got to where I could stand the constant ringing," Elmer said. "But now all I get is a busy signal and it's driving me nuts."

A man is as good as he has to be; a woman as bad as she dares.

The young fellow was terribly bashful and yet he desperately wanted to marry the girl. Finally, he blurted, "Dearest one, would you like to be buried with my people?"

There is a family in Salem, Illinois, that had eight children, all of them girls. But, wonder of wonders, the ninth baby was a boy and the father had himself a week-long celebration. Toward the end of the happy time, a friend asked the father whom the boy looked like, Papa or Mama. And the proud Papa answered, "We haven't looked at his face yet."

Whenever a husband and wife begin to discuss their marriage, they are giving evidence at an inquest.

H. L. Mencken

Sarah and Julius were both overweight in spite of repeated dieting, weight-losing classes and all kinds of diet foods and fads. She was losing confidence in their ability to reduce their weight. "I'm beginning to think," she told Julius, "the only way a woman can get a youthful figure is to ask her how old she is."

At the inquest for her late husband, the widow asked if she recalled her husband's last words. She thought a few moments, then said, "Yes, I do recall him saying something like, 'I don't see how in heck they can make money out of this booze when they sell a bottle of it for a buck-and-a-half!'"

Wife: "We are not going to the mountains and that's final. The air out there disagrees with me."
Husband: "My dear, it wouldn't dare."

A famous manufacturer of mustard had presented to him, by the advertising department, a new billboard that showed a young husband eating in a high-class restaurant. A lovely waitress was standing beside him, holding out a bottle of their brand of mustard. Everyone thought it a great advertisement with only one problem, the printing on the image read: "What Does She Know About Your Husband That You Don't Know?" And that was the rub, the one thing the reviewing committee criticized, saying it was entirely too suggestive. So they changed the wordage to read, "Since He Gets It At The Shopping Center, Why Not Give It To Him At Home."

"JUST HOW LONG IS THE DOCTOR GOING TO KEEP YOU ON THIS EGG DIET?"

In his high-rise, Peter Jenkins was taking the elevator to his apartment. On the tenth floor, an entirely nude woman got on the elevator and Pete was so confused at the sight of her, that all he could think to say was, "My wife upstairs has a costume exactly like yours."

There's a sign on the receptionist's desk in a planned parenthood office that reads, "CONTRACEPTIONIST."

Mary Jo Saner was describing her new apartment to her mother: "Mom, you've got to come and see it. It's gorgeous! Great sitting room and the bedroom is exquisite. The kitchen is a model of efficiency and the bathroom...well, all I can say is...the bathroom is out of this world!"

There was a pause, then her mother remarked, "Isn't that a little inconvenient?"

The obstetrician remarked, "Y'now...too darned often people hold the stork responsible for a situation that might better be laid at the claws of a lark."

♥ ☆ ♥ ☆ ♥

The young fellow came running into the office where he passed out cigars saying, "Congratulate me. It's a girl. 'Five foot two, eyes of blue and she weighs one hundred and two.'"

♥ ☆ ♥ ☆ ♥

A guy in New York owned a simple, unpretentious restaurant and became very angry when the Internal Revenue Service sent two agents to examine his income tax return. "I'm a simple guy, run a modest restaurant and here you guys are wanting to question my return. I don't understand it."

"Well, you claimed deductions for six trips to Florida that you and your family took. We wondered how vacations could be business expenses," the agent said.

"Simple enough. Did you ever stop to figure that we deliver?"

The eighty-year-old couple were discussing how to entertain two new friends, a couple of their own age whom they had just met. "But what will we do with them, dear?" said the wife. "How will we entertain them?"

"Well, let's see," her husband said, wrinkling his brow in thought, "we could...we...sure, that's it, we could show them our collection of Metamucil."

It's amazing how active pre-marriage life can be...and how all that activity is cut in half after marriage. For example, we do a lot of billing and cooing before marriage. But afterwards, it's cut in half! The cooing ends but not the billing!

♥ ☆ ♥ ☆ ♥

Martha Boykin was a bit prudish. She thought that **vice versa** meant dirty poems!

♥ ☆ ♥ ☆ ♥

A first-time Congressman was being interviewed by the local paper. "Mr. Congressman," said the reporter, "when you get to Washington, are you going to be a pawn for the powerful interests that most of your constituents think will control you?"

"I resent that question, Sir," the Congressman replied. "I do not plan to take my wife to Washington."

♥ ☆ ♥ ☆ ♥

Isn't it strange that while brides are dressed in white to show their purity, the groom wears black?

♥ ☆ ♥ ☆ ♥

Returning from the funeral of his mother-in-law, he and his wife were frightened when a brick fell from a nearby building and crashed on the hood of their car. "Dear, your mother made it to heaven!"

♥ ☆ ♥ ☆ ♥

Today it is wise and perfectly acceptable to have your children properly spaced. That's usually about ten feet apart.

Edgar had been married three years and there was trouble in the family. So he decided to talk to his father and get the old man's advice on how to handle the situation.

"Dad, things aren't going so well in my house. For one thing, I forgot my wife's birthday. How can I keep from repeating that? My wife was furious."

"About that, you don't have to worry. If you forget it once, it'll never happen again!"

♥ ☆ ♥ ☆ ♥

Mrs. Abrams went to the psychiatrist about her son. "What seems to be the problem with him, Madam?" the psychiatrist asked.

"All day long, he blows bubbles! Takes a pipe and blows soap bubbles. All day long, he does this."

"Well, that seems not so serious, Ma'am," the doctor said. "Lots of kids blow bubbles."

"Well, I sure think it's odd," the mother said. "And so does his wife."

♥ ☆ ♥ ☆ ♥

Retirement means twice as much husband for half as much money.

♥ ☆ ♥ ☆ ♥

The mother read, in a book on how to raise children, that the father and mother ought not to hide their bodies from their children, that the kids ought to grow up feeling that all parts of the body were acceptable as trees and flowers and such, and should be taken for granted. So the mother took the little girl into the bathtub with her only to have the child remark, "Mama, how come I'm so plain and you're so fancy?"

♥ ☆ ♥ ☆ ♥

If you have an attic filled with generations of family memorabilia, never send a nostalgic person to clean it out.

♥ ☆ ♥ ☆ ♥

After four divorces, disillusioned Elmer Sludge defined marital life in just three words:
1. Matrimony
2. Acrimony
3. Alimony

" HOW DID THE AUDIT GO, DEAR? "

Susan Epplewaite was going down the street, pushing her baby carriage, when she met a friend she hadn't seen for several years. After their tearful greeting, the friend said, "But Susie, I didn't know you were married."

"I'm not," Susie replied. "But I ain't been neglected."

In olden times, sacrifices were made at the altar -- a practice which is still very much practiced.

Helen Rowland

"Hey, Baby," laughed the attractive wife of banker Joe Thomas, "I've got the best surprise for little ol' you and it'll tickle you half to death."

"Great! And I can't thank you enough, Honey, for such gorgeous consideration."

"You wait and see," she said. "Just wait here for a moment until I try it on!"

"Darling," Flora Belfast said to her husband at breakfast, "I never really felt that I had aged until this morning when I put my brassiere on backward and it fit better that way."

"I had the same kind of experience," her husband replied. "Remember when the kids told us what they were studying in history? Well, later, I realized that those were current events when I was a kid."

♥ ☆ ♥ ☆ ♥

She had been unmarried for most of her life, then, suddenly, she got married and told everybody, "I've been **dismissed**."

♥ ☆ ♥ ☆ ♥

A country preacher once observed that marriage is a lot like farming. If you want it to work, you've got to give it constant attention, seven days and nights every week.

♥ ☆ ♥ ☆ ♥

MARITAL DEFINITIONS

Engagement:	A call to arms. Hence as day follows night, divorce is disarmament.
Grass widow:	The wife of a dead vegetarian.
Love:	A quest.
Marriage:	A conquest.
Divorce:	An inquest.
Mrs.:	The title of a job entailing heavy, heavy duty with mighty poor earnings.
Obedient wife:	One whose husband tells her to do what she wants to...and who does it.
Remarriage:	The triumph of hope over experience. *Samuel Johnson*
Matrimony:	A knot tied by a preacher but untied by a lawyer.
Marriage:	Said by some to be not a word but a sentence.
Light Housekeeping:	One canned thing after another.
Wedlock:	A lock with the key thrown away. (Today, add "Half the time.")

There's a story going the rounds in Illinois about a guy whose wife demanded that he get rid of a mouse that was driving her to distraction. So he bought a mousetrap, went to get cheese but didn't have any. No problem. He put a picture of cheese, cut from a magazine, in the trap as bait. He heard the trap snap that evening, went to the basement and saw in the trap...a **picture** of a mouse.

Two old friends were discussing the desirability of marriage. "Do you honestly believe it's better than being single?" one asked. "Yeah, I really do," responded the other. "If it weren't for being married, I'd have to do all my fighting with strangers."

Ah, Divorce! "Tis almost as common as marriage, alas!"

Edna Mae had been housecleaning all day and she was tired, dirty and out-of-sorts. When husband Peter came home and saw her, he said, "Edna, you're pretty dirty, you know."
Edna replied, "I'm even prettier clean."

♥ ☆ ♥ ☆ ♥

There's no question that insanity is hereditary...parents get it from their kids.

♥ ☆ ♥ ☆ ♥

Bert and Sarah Tingle were both ninety years old when they decided to seek a divorce. When they appeared before the attorney to arrange things, he asked, "Allow me a question, folks. Please tell me why you waited so long...I think you said you'd been married sixty years...to seek a divorce?"
"Well, Sir," Bert said. "We thought we had best wait until our children were all dead."

"Marriage is a great institution but I'm not ready for an institution yet."

Mae West

At the county fair, Johnny Forsythe stepped on a weighing scale, put in a quarter and got his weight plus a card that read: "You are intelligent, strong and handsome, have a fine character and are a leader among men. The opposite sex finds you attractive."

Johnny's wife read the card and remarked: "And the weight is wrong, too."

Ferdinand had been widowed twice and stated in his will that he wished to be buried between the two women. He added this stipulation: "Please bury me between them, but tilt me bit toward Mary."

Have you heard that germs can be passed from one person to another on dollar bills? Well, that is simply not true because nothing, but nothing, could live on a dollar.

♥ ☆ ♥ ☆ ♥

Eddie Hagen told his wife that for the rest of his life, he was at her disposal. She replied, "Eddie, that's a lot of garbage!"

"Tell me, Mrs. Myers..." the doctor asked, "did your husband take two of the pills I gave him, each day, and follow that with a swig of whiskey?"

"Doctor, he's a leetle bit behind in his pills, but a month ahead on whiskey!"

♥ ☆ ♥ ☆ ♥

Judge:	"Can we have your name, please?"
Defendant:	"Mary Stokes."
Judge:	"Are you married?"
Defendant:	"Yes, Sir, sure am."
Judge:	"Occupation of your husband?"
Defendant:	"Manufacturer."
Judge:	"Children?"
Defendant:	"Certainly not! Furniture!"

♥ ☆ ♥ ☆ ♥

I snuck upstairs with shoes in hand
    When the night itself took wing,
And saw my wife up ahead of me,
    Doing the same damned thing.

Pete Myers had been a paratrooper in the big war. One evening at a party, he was asked how many successful parachute jumps he had made in the war.

"I can answer that for you," his wife replied. "All of them."

Two gossips were discussing their neighbors down the street. "They're a perfectly matched pair," one old girl said. "She's a hypochondriac and he's a perfect pill."

Everyone is familiar with the Hatfields and the Coys of Kentucky. Well, one of the Hatfields came into town and went to the doctor. "Come and have a look at mah son-in-law," he asked the doctor. "He ain't been worth a dang since I shot him last Monday."

"I know that you Hatfields are might quick on the draw," said the country doctor. "But I never knew one of you to shoot someone from your own family."

"Ah know, ah know," the Hatfield said. "But y'see when I done shot him, he waren't my son-in-law."

.DLETCH.

"THE DEPARTMENT STORE ON THE CORNER HAS HAD TO TAKE A CHAPTER 11 BANKRUPTCY. I FELT SO SORRY FOR THEM I DECIDED TO HELP."

The first part of our marriage was just great. Then, on the way back from the church... .

The waiter felt very uncomfortable watching the elderly couple eat. It seems that the husband was eating away at the big dinner but the poor wife was just sitting there looking forlorn and hungry. "Aren't you hungry, Ma'am?" the waiter asked her.

"You dern betcha I'm hungry," she replied. "But I got to wait for him to get finished with our teeth!"

"Daddy, tell me about yourself. When does old age start for a man?"

"Well, let me see now...him-m-m...Well, I guess you could say that old age begins for a guy when he starts to give good advice instead of setting a bad example."

♥ ☆ ♥ ☆ ♥

"I was sorry to hear that you had lost your husband, Mrs. Isham."

"Thank you. And it was quite a surprise. We didn't at all expect it. He was only ninety-two years old."

"Ninety-two? But that was a marvelous and long life. Why was everybody surprised?"

"Because his parachute didn't open."

Someone has wisely remarked that the bonds of matrimony are a good investment only when the **interest** is high and sustained.

♥ ☆ ♥ ☆ ♥

Mr. and Mrs. Joachim were asked the secret of their longevity. They were each ninety years old.

"Well, we attribute our long life to the fact that neither of us smoke or drink. We walk three miles a day, get to bed at nine o'clock and eat a well-balanced diet."

"So that's it. But I had an uncle and aunt who lived exactly the same way and they died at sixty and sixty-two. How do you explain that?"

"Well, h-mmm, I'd say they just didn't keep it up long enough."

♥ ☆ ♥ ☆ ♥

One way for a big woman to attract widespread attention is to wear slacks in public.

"George, I hate to have you go out on the highway and drive to town. There are just too many cars!"

"I know it, Mary. But the good side to it is that today there's a lot fewer horse thieves."

The suggestion has been made that preachers could get more husbands to church if they'd have beautiful ushers, as comely as airline hostesses. Obviously, the wives would then go along for security's sake.

Mary Peters was reading a book on the ancient land of Egypt. "Ed," she said to her husband, "do you know that it took them over a hundred years to build a single pyramid? Isn't that remarkable?"

Ed Peters: "Yeah, it sure is. But y'know something...I think they must have used the same contractor who remodeled our kitchen."

Dan and Sally invested a good deal of money in a magical potion that claimed to make people smarter. But they could see no change in one another and so went back to the flim-flam artist who had sold the stuff to them. "We've been on this potion for six months," Dan complained to the guy, "and we can't see that your medicine made us a darned bit smarter."

"Ah, but you are," the crook said. "If you've observed that much, you are a whole lot smarter than when you bought it."

Husband: "Dear, I bought you a poity boid for your birthday."
Wife: "Gee, thanks, Dear. But they're not 'boids', they're 'birds.'"
Husband: "Yeah? Well, dey sure looks like boids."

♥ ☆ ♥ ☆ ♥

Wife: "Can we go to Cousin Lucy's fortieth birthday party next week?"
Husband: "Why not? Don't we go every year?"

♥ ☆ ♥ ☆ ♥

Marriage is an adventure, like going to war.

G. K. Chesteron

A suburban lady who was not only disagreeable but also an arrogant snob, was talking with her neighbor.

"We'll soon be in a much better neighborhood," she said.

"We, too," replied the neighbor.

"Oh, you're also moving?" the snob asked.

"Nope," said the neighbor, grinning, "we're staying right here."

And Larry Kyle says that the two of them, Mary and he, have determined never to get too nostalgic about anything for fear that it might come back.

When asked by his wife what he would like from her for Christmas, he replied, "Why don't you get me a seven-piece fishing outfit...a rod and a six-pack."

Farmer George White was not overly gifted with intelligence. When the man from the highway department came to his home, located on ten acres of pasture, to tell him that the new highway would pass through his land, he was furious. "Louise, it ain't right," George told his wife, "it just ain't right that they're gonna run a four-lane highway through our pasture. Every dang time a car comes along, I'll have to go down and open the gate."

Norman and Polly rarely ate out. But this one time they decided to do it right and went to the finest restaurant in town. The next day their neighbor asked how they liked the food. "We never did get any," Normal said. "We waited for someone to tell us where to sit and nobody came, so we left."

"I don't understand that," the neighbor said.

"Well, there was a big sign where we entered that read, 'PLEASE WAIT FOR THE HOSTESS TO BE SEATED.' And that hostess never did sit down!"

Mary Kyle says that life is lots better now that she and the mister have decided that what they have is better than what they are missing.

"HE'S TALKING ABOUT GRAMPA."

"Mary, they told Alex that he had to get more exercise, that he's so out-of-shape that if he didn't get more exercise, it would shorten his life."

"And what did Alex do about it?"

"Scared him so much that he decided to roll his own cigarettes."

It seems indubitably true that the most dangerous years for a marriage are...the first, second, third, fourth...and subsequent years.

Jean Kerr once observed that a lawyer is never entirely satisfied with a divorce that ends amicably, anymore than a mortician would want, after completing the job, to have the body sit up on the table!

They say that the divorce laws of Nevada are so liberal that, out there, women don't cry at their weddings.

Herb Block used to say that if groceries at the supermarket got any more expensive, he'd carry his money to the market in a shopping cart and his groceries home in his briefcase.

Freda and Adolph Hassen were on a senior citizens' tour of the Art Institute of Chicago. The guide was explaining the various groupings of art. When they came to an African exhibit, the guide asked to be excused for a few moments. So Freda and Adolph wandered around the exhibit but stopped before a strange, if familiar carved wooden object.

"How odd," Freda said, "I wonder what they call it?"

"It's obviously African," Adolph said. "I think it's called a phallic symbol."

"Well," Freda said, "I'd hate to tell you what it looks like."

Having recently become the beneficiary of a rich, if miserly, uncle who was worth a lot of money, David Echter said, "I never much cared for my Uncle...he was too miserly. But I can tell you this, for sure, misers make wonderful ancestors."

"You ask about my son, George?" Jimmy Jones responded to his friend. "Well, let me put it this way. Some men are willing to work and others are willing to let them. George is in the latter class."

"I hear the Alonzos got a divorce. What was the trouble? Incompatibility?"

"Only the first two syllables of that last word!"

Charlie and Mabel Proctor were showing some friends the photographs taken on a recent hunting trip.

"Why they are beautiful!" one of their friends exclaimed.

"Aren't they though!" Charlie agreed.

"But you should have seen how much better our daughter did," Mabel said, "she bagged a young attorney with a huge law practice."

What did the electrician's wife say to her husband when he came in at 2 A.M.?

"Wire you insulate, Dear?"

♥ ☆ ♥ ☆ ♥

A man was caught, tried and jailed for being a shill with stolen goods. But the cops couldn't find half the stuff and he wouldn't tell them where he had hid it. Then one day he got a letter from his wife saying, "It's time to dig the garden, but since you're in jail, there's no one to do it. Looks like I'll have to do it myself."

"Don't do it," he wrote her, "that's where I buried all the loot the cops are after. So don't touch that old garden plot." He handed the letter to the jailer to mail for him.

Soon, he got another letter from his wife. "The other day a truckload of cops came to the house and dug up the entire garden. What shall I do?"

"Plant the garden!" wrote the shrewd guy.

♥ ☆ ♥ ☆ ♥

Someone once said that alimony is "the billing minus the cooing."

♥ ☆ ♥ ☆ ♥

Two avid fishermen were discussing the sport. "I really enjoy the fresh air and all. Being alone with nature, trying to outsmart the fish, hooking and landing a big one. It's the most thrilling thing I do. But tell me, why do you fish?"

"That's easy to answer," the other replied. "My son is learning to play the trumpet."

♥ ☆ ♥ ☆ ♥

Remember...an engagement is merely an option on a life sentence.

♥ ☆ ♥ ☆ ♥

How's this for the opening lines in a divorce attorney's newspaper advertisement: "We guarantee you satisfaction or...your honey back."

♥ ☆ ♥ ☆ ♥

Peter and Martha Jennings are parents of a young lady who is President of the Mothers-and-Mini-Skirt Club. They are thinking of renaming the group The Daughters of the American Revelation.

176

He was a first-class snob, always bragging about his ancestors who came over on the Mayflower. "I suppose you'll be telling us your people were with Noah on the ark!" his wife sneered. "Now that you mention it," the braggart replied, "a distant grandfather complained that Noah never did return the hammer he borrowed."

"Mary, is that new dress torn? Or am I seeing things?"
"Both."

"I'm really angry, Elmer," his wife screamed at him. "I've been holding dinner for you for two hours. Where on earth have you been?"
"I've been standing in the lake, waiting for it to get dark," he replied.
"Why on earth would you do a silly thing like that?" she asked.
"I lost my swimming trunks."

The president of the Equal Rights Convention announced, "We have for our speakers tonight, Mr. and Mrs. Delbert Schroeder...not necessarily in that order."

Margie Emmerson wanted a certain jazz record, so she dialed a record shop but got the wrong number. A man responded from a carpentry shop. Totally unaware of the mistake, Margie asked, "Do you have 'Eyes of Blue and a Love That's True?'"
"Nope," said the carpenter. "But I do have a wife and twelve kids in Iowa."

What do they call a man with twelve or more kids? A fresh heir fiend.

He had sworn to marry never,
    She was set on being a bride,
Surely you know the answer,
    She had nature on her side.

"Edward, tomorrow is our fiftieth wedding anniversary and we've planned not a thing. What do you think we should do?"
"Let's celibate."

♥ ☆ ♥ ☆ ♥

Judging from testimony heard these days in divorce courts, one would think people got married by an injustice of the peace.

♥ ☆ ♥ ☆ ♥

Polly Simmons and Greta Samson were attending a Bible class. When class dismissed, they walked home and discussed the day's Old Testament lesson.

"That Old King Solomon was sure a mighty patient guy," Polly said, "putting up with all those wives and concubines! Gosh, but it must have taken a dozen supermarkets to supply food for all those women."

"Somehow, I'm not interested in what he fed those women of his," Greta replied, "I can't help wondering what **he** was eating!"

♥ ☆ ♥ ☆ ♥

One definition for alimony is..."All of my money."

"GUESS WHAT? STANLEY HAS LEARNED TO USE THE TELEPHONE."

Kisses are dandy in sustaining a marriage...but a shrug now and then, when each discovers a failing in the other, sure does help.

There's an ancient story still circulating around the Tennessee hill country about a backwoodsman who found a mirror that someone -- a tourist -- probably had lost. He took a good look in it, saying, "I'll be dadblamed if it ain't my old Paw. I never knew he'd had his pickshur took." He took the mirror home and hid it in the attic. But his wife had grown suspicious of all that rumbling up there and when the old boy left the house, she went to the attic, hunted around and found the mirror. She looked into it, then remarked, "So, that's the old biddy he's been chasin'!"

Are you among those of an age to recall when folks sat down to eat dinner and counted their blessing...not calories?

There was an interesting typo in the newsletter mailed to members of the OLD COUPLES BRIDGE CLUB. It read, "Margie and Ben Upjohn's granddaughter is getting married next month. As you can imagine, she's terribly busy getting her torso ready."

♥ ☆ ♥ ☆ ♥

Shakespeare said, "There's a divinity that shapes our ends, rough-hew them how we will." But in our time, it's a girdle that does it!

♥ ☆ ♥ ☆ ♥

Mary Tompkins advised her daughter about the kind of dresses she should wear. "My dear," she said, "I follow the advice of a famous Hollywood dress designer who said, 'Wear dresses that are tight enough to show you are a woman and loose enough to show you are a lady.'"

♥ ☆ ♥ ☆ ♥

Do you have trouble getting your children's attention? Here's the solution; just sit down and look comfortable.

The young man and his wife were in the courtroom, airing their troubles during their divorce suit. "We were quite happy for two years, your Honor," the girl moaned, "and then the baby came."

"Oh," the Judge said, uncertain of the meaning of her statement. "Boy or girl?" he asked.

"It was a ... ." but the girl broke down and sobbed while the Judge waited for her to pull herself together. When she seemed better, the Judge asked, "I asked you if it was a boy or girl."

"It was a girl, of course," the poor woman sobbed. "And she moved in right next door to us."

"And for how long do you expect to stay with your new job?" the new bride was asked. She replied, "From here to maternity."

Jelly is a food commonly found on kids, bread and piano keys.

Two women were discussing their neighbor, a woman notorious for the gossip she spread. "I hate to talk about others," one of the women said, "but I was told that after she returned from her vacation at the beach, her tongue was sunburned."

Henry and his wife, Mary, dearly loved their daughter. They bought her an expensive bikini for her birthday. It was the least they could give her.

Dean Noon was a bit over 70 and very wealthy, when he took a two-week Florida vacation. When he returned, he was accompanied by a lovely young lady, curvaceous and vivacious.

"Where did you find her?" a friend asked. "I'm not sure," the old fellow replied. "I just opened my wallet and there she was."

The wisest couple in a small Midwestern town were attending a lecture titled, "The Causes of Marital Strife." One was listening, and the other was keeping his mouth shut.

A just-divorced woman stormed out of the courtroom and went for a walk along the lake when she spotted a bottle on the shore. She took it, opened it, and out jumped a genie. "Sure appreciate your releasing me from that bottle," the genie said. "For that favor, I'll grant you three wishes. But remember that for your every wish, your former husband gets double."

"I want a Lincoln car," said the woman.

"Granted. But your husband gets two Lincolns."

"Now I want a million dollars for my second wish."

"Here it is. But your husband got two million."

"For my third and last wish, I would like to be half dead."

Franny Feuer claims that planning her recent anniversary was easy...a piece of cake.

John and Mary Edgar checked into a Las Vegas hotel and asked for something restful and pleasant for the night under $300. They were given two sleeping pills.

♥ ☆ ♥ ☆ ♥

Be careful in selecting a wedding cake because some of them can give you indigestion the rest of your life.

♥ ☆ ♥ ☆ ♥

Talk about large families! There was this huge family in the little town of Athens, Illinois. They had so many kids that the county school board decided to build the new school next door to them.

♥ ☆ ♥ ☆ ♥

The couple stood before the clerk at the marriage bureau, waiting to receive their license. The girl remarked, "It certainly seems odd to be asking for a license **after** the hunting season has ended."

♥ ☆ ♥ ☆ ♥

Paul Fisher looked at his income tax return and sighed. "Y'know something, Edna," he said to his wife, "if Patrick Henry hated taxation without representation, he should be here today to see how lousy it is **with** representation."

**"Oh alright, if that's the way you feel about it,
_I'LL_ change her diapers"**

Definition of divorce: What couples can agree on when they disagree on everything else.

♥ ☆ ♥ ☆ ♥

Someone has defined a credit card thus: What you use today to buy something you won't be able to afford tomorrow because you will still be paying for yesterday.

♥ ☆ ♥ ☆ ♥

They always tell me to smile, to always smile in time of crisis and real trouble. Well, it seems to me that the man who can smile at such a time has suddenly thought of someone on whom to lay the blame for it all!

♥ ☆ ♥ ☆ ♥

There's a rumor out that our first lady, Eve, said to Adam, "Don't be a fool. Of course the kids look like you!"

The wealthy father was chatting with his daughter's fiance, kind of sizing him up, and asked the young fellow, "Would you still care and love my little girl if you suddenly discovered we were poor?" The young man responded, "You bet I would...even more..I'd love her just as much if you didn't have a nickel to your name."

"So much for that," the father replied. "The wedding is canceled because we've got enough fools in the family now!"

A salesman showed up at work with a terrible black eye, saying he got it by trying to end a vicious argument between a man and wife. His fellow worker said, "Well, that's what a feller gets for dipping his spoon in another man's soup."

A sure sign to tell if a guy is married to the girl is to notice the way he honks at her.

The early part of our marriage, things went just fine and then on our way out of the church...!

It's tough to teach kids the alphabet these days. Most of them think that V follows T.

Ed Dryfoose bought a cornet and was trying to learn to play it. He was busy practicing one day when the phone rang. "I'm your next-door neighbor," the lady said, "and my husband is home sick. Do you know your noise is making things worse?"

"No," said Ed, "but if you'll hum a few bars, I think I can fake it for you."

"Florence, you really made me angry tonight."

"Oh dear, I'm sorry. What did I do?"

"You just the same as told everybody how old I was when you announced that we had a five percent mortgage on the house."

Adam and Naomi were deeply in love and had a date almost every night. They were engaged and Adam usually let Naomi make all their decisions...where to go of an evening, what to eat, this, that, and the other thing.

Adam was a salesman at a furniture store...and not too bright. Naomi was a bookkeeper.

One night, when Adam came to call on Naomi, he found her almost voiceless with laryngitis. So Adam asked what she'd like to do that night. She drew a picture of a steak and they had a dandy. Then he asked, "What would you like to do now?" And she drew a picture of a dish of ice cream and that's what they had. Then he asked, "What would you like to do now?" And she drew a picture of a bed. "Now honey," he said, heatedly, "this is not the time for us to be visiting the furniture store!"

It's true that a fool and his money are soon parted but...the rest of us manage to get the same results in the supermarkets and discount stores.

The exercise that can most affect your life is walking down the aisle.

Many cases of divorce are really more on the order of anti-trust cases.

Prosecuting Attorney: "Mrs. Rosen, would you tell the jury why you shot your husband with a bow and arrow?"

Mrs. Rosen: "Well, you see, hm-m-m, Sir, well, I didn't want to wake the baby."

"Did you hear that Susie Flynn's husband was arrested for early shopping for Christmas?"

"Really? But there's no law against that!"

"Sure there is...he was shopping before the store opened."

How's this for the unintended truth: "Honey, I've taught our boy everything I know and he's still an ignoramus."

Mrs. Susie Snodgrass is so prim and proper that when she goes to the store for toilet paper, she asks for "the bathroom stationery."

A truism: Setting a good example for your kids sure takes all the fun out of middle age.

Wife: "It's a good thing you're an accountant, Mike."
Mike: "Why do you say that?"
Wife: "Because I want you to account for coming home at four A.M."

Edith Tonkin was at the check-out desk of the supermarket with a shopping cart piled high with groceries that she and her husband had selected. She took out a twenty-dollar bill and remarked, while looking at it, "Maurice, it is certainly true that appearances are deceiving. This twenty-dollar bill looks exactly like the one we used twenty years ago."

The young groom was quite certain that he didn't want to spend the rest of his life in pursuit of money. "Money isn't everything," he told his new bride. "I'm looking for other, more important things."
"Well, Sweetheart," the bride replied. "More power to you. But I want to assure you of one thing...money may not be everything, but it's miles and miles ahead of whatever is in second place."

♥ ☆ ♥ ☆ ♥

If you ask a kid to describe a balanced diet, he'll probably tell you it's having a hamburger in both hands.

♥ ☆ ♥ ☆ ♥

An old maid: A woman who was engaged once too seldom.
Fred Allen

Roger Grauman seemed never to get his car paid for. "I'm convinced of one thing," Roger said, "and that is...drive-in banks were established so the true owner of a car can have a chance to see it now and then."

Some kids are spoiled rotten because it's considered bad taste to spank grandmas.

Ella Saunders was busy in the kitchen when she heard a child screaming out in front of her house. She ran to the door, looked out, saw a little child on the sidewalk screaming loud enough to wake a Cuban...in Cuba. She rushed to the child who sobbed and said between groans, "I tripped on that broken place in y-y-your sidewalk."

"Now, child, you must be strong and manly about this. Don't cry."

"Don't cry she tells me. Sister, I'm gonna sue the hell out of somebody over this."

"How do you feel about Plannned Parenthood?"

There's an ancient story that is still a dandy, like all good stories. It seems that a pregnant girl went to see her obstetrician who asked her, "And how many babies do you have now, Mrs. Senzell?"

"This'll be my twelfth," the young woman replied.

"Goodness gracious," he exclaimed, "you do multiply rabbitly, don't you!"

A young lady, about to graduate from college, went to church one Sunday and this is what she prayed: "Lord, I don't ask You for much. But I really mean it this time...would You please, please, please send my mother a son-in-law."

A man sought a divorce for a most unusual reason. It seems he loved to sleep on their waterbed. But his stubborn wife refused to trim her long toenails!

Father: "I'm sure glad that you studied accounting in school, Mary."
Mary: "Why is that, Dad?"
Father: "Because I want you to account for coming home at 3:00 a.m. this morning."

If you've ever had a baby, you know that child-care is learned from the bottom up.

There were eighteen children in this devout Catholic family, and they were having a hard time finding enough to eat. A social worker called on the mother, asked many questions, and finally remarked, "Mrs. Jenkins, have you ever heard of the rhythm method of birth control?"

"Of course, I have. All of us practice it. Ten of my kids have musical instruments, but who wants to get a band together at three o'clock in the morning?"

A young wife, about to have her fifth child, went to her doctor and was told about the proper care of her breasts.

"I don't plan to nurse this baby, Doctor," she said, "I'm going to use a good commercial formula for milk."

The doctor talked and talked and finally convinced her that she should breast-feed the coming baby. "Well, Doctor, I see the wisdom in what you've been saying. But far more than that...if I got to carry both of them around, I must just as well use them."

Domestic harmony: A condition brought on when the husband plays second fiddle and yet pays the piper.

An obstetrician is said to have read these lines at a political meeting:
> Hurrah for the stork,
> A terrific, white bird
> That nests in residential districts.
> He sings us no tunes
> Doesn't yield us fine plumes,
> But sure helps on those vital statistics.

Bridegroom: A gent who exchanges living **quarters** for a better **half**.

Those who say they "sleep like a baby" haven't got one.

Then there was the couple who had just been blessed with their first child, a girl. The announcement read: WE HAVE SKIRTED THE ISSUE.

Little Eddie Foy, eight years old, interrupted his mother's bridge game with an excited, "Hey, Mom. Didn't I hear you tell Aunt Katie that our new baby had dad's eyes and your complexion?"

"Yes, Eddie. I did say that."

"Well, then, Mom, you better go take another look. You forgot Grandpa. The baby's got Grandpa's teeth."

A sure way to keep your kids on track is to use normal switching facilities.

It's a beautiful day in the park and a young father is pushing a baby carriage in which a baby is screaming his head off. And as the father wheels the baby along, he keeps murmuring, "Easy now, Donald. Just keep calm, Donald, steady boy. It's all right, Donald. Just relax, Donald. It's gonna be all right, Donald..."

And a mother passes by and says to the guy pushing the carriage, "You certainly know how to talk to an upset child --quietly and gently." And she leans over the carriage and says, "What seems to be the trouble, Donald?"

And the father says, "Oh, no. He's Henry. I'm Donald."

♥ ☆ ♥ ☆ ♥

This business of raising children is rather like playing golf because you always think you'll do better the next time around.

♥ ☆ ♥ ☆ ♥

The newlyweds had just gotten into their hotel room, when the bride picked up the phone, and asked Room Service to send up a television set.

"A TV set," growled the groom. "Why do we need a television set on our wedding night?"

"But, honey," she explained, "every now and then we'll have to get **some** relaxation!"

♥ ☆ ♥ ☆ ♥

Tom Harvey's wife is so depressed, so down-in-the-dumps that she actually reads the obituary column to cheer herself up.

♥ ☆ ♥ ☆ ♥

The complete life cycle of a contemporary marriage goes about like this:

"Charlie and Suzanne were deeply in love and then they were married. They lived happily ever after for several months."

♥ ☆ ♥ ☆ ♥

The old-timers used to say that the factory or enterprise that produces the most useful and important product is the home.

These same old-timers considered folks who saved money as close-fisted and even misers. Today they call them miracle workers.

♥ ☆ ♥ ☆ ♥

Pete and Clara were very much in favor of sex education in the schools. That is, they were until their daughter came home with an A in the subject.

♥ ☆ ♥ ☆ ♥

Norma Jean and Tom Patton were avid home gardeners. Recently, they subscribed to a new magazine on horticulture: WEEDER'S DIGEST.

♥ ☆ ♥ ☆ ♥

Puns from the PAN AMERICAN NEWSLETTER, a bunch of pun-fanciers you knighted to offer (far, far off) some of the best pun-ches ever delivered on a pun-ching bag.

It's not the 1:00 A.M. feeding that bothers me. It's the 1:00 A.M. feuding as to whose turn it is to tackle the 2:00 A.M. feeding.

Some doctors say the practice of circumcision is petering out.

Urologist: A doctor who helps you when you feel too much peer pressure.

The most litigious of all lawyers are those from Sioux City.

♥ ☆ ♥ ☆ ♥

Hill county Kentuckians still make moonshine and sell it. Well, this particular 'shiner' made a batch for his son, a new husband. The young man protested that the last batch of 'shine' was too strong.

"Well if it was too strong, you shouldn't have drunk it, Son," the moonshiner said.

"Oh, I drank it all right, Pa. But now, every time I sneeze, I burn a hole in our furniture."

♥ ☆ ♥ ☆ ♥

Did you hear about the girlie magazine published by the MEN'S FIDELITY CLUB? It has the same girl as the centerfold month after month after month.

♥ ☆ ♥ ☆ ♥

"Bill, Doctor George called today. He said your check came back."

"That makes it even-stephen! My arthritis came back, too."

190

"Hi, Mary, and just how is hubby George?"

"Oh, he's just fine, Sarah. He looks swell. You know, he's been taking a medicine called Eternal Youth Elixir, and it seems to be keeping him young."

"Oh, Mary, you should know better. That has to be a swindle. There's no such thing as eternal youth. I bet he's spent a bundle on that thimble-rigger's game."

"You bet he has...he's been taking it for two hundred years."

"Peter, did you keep your appointment with the doctor today?"

"Yeah, I went there but I left almost at once."

"What? Why did you do such a thing?"

"Well, I saw that the plants in his office were wilting and dying."

There is a suggestion now before the courts that asks the wedding ceremonial words be changed from the traditional "I do" to "Perhaps."

"WAS THE CHILI TOO HOT, MALCOLM?"

There is absolutely nothing that confirms one's belief in heredity more than having a handsome child.

Sara Feuer returned from a bridge party to tell her husband that she had learned an important truth while playing. "Let me tell you this, Honey," she said to him. "Gossip is that which enters both ears and emerges from the mouth enlarged twenty times!"

Down in Alabama, Sissie Murphy worked in the Montgomery Glove Factory Office where she had been employed for thirty years. One day she went to the boss and asked to have the afternoon off to take her son to the doctor.

"But, Sissie," he said, "I thought you were an old maid."

"Yessir, ah am," she said. "But I ain't the fussy kind."

Edna Seamon's husband had passed on and she was so distraught that she sought out a spiritualist who told her that her husband was fine, that he was eagerly awaiting a reunion with her. "Is there anything he needs?" Edna asked.

The spiritualist went into a transient state, then replied, "He says he'd love a package of cigarettes."

"I'll send them immediately," Edna said joyfully. "But did he give an address?"

"No. But he didn't ask for matches."

"Hey, Dad," the boy asked, "can you tell me how wars get started?"

"Look at it this way, son," the father began. "Let us say that England and America got into a dangerous quarrel... ."

"But England and America aren't anywhere near a quarrel," interrupted Mother.

"I didn't say they were," Pop replied. "I was just using a hypothetical example."

"Stupid! Ridiculous! Unwarranted!" yelled Mother.

"It is not stupid or ridiculous at all," Father shouted. "The kid'll be forever a fool if he listens to you."

"Hold it down, hold it down," their son cautioned. "I think I know now how wars get started. Thanks a lot for the information."

Katie Myers had spent the entire day trying to clean out her attic. Late that afternoon, she came down out of it and remarked to her husband: "Nobody who can read at all well is ever successful at cleaning out an attic."

U.S. Senator Zebulon B. Vance, his wife, and other senators and their wives, were invited to an outing on Chesapeake Bay. As they climbed aboard the ship, Senator Vance happened to look up and was given a view beneath the skirts of the lady who was mounting ahead of him.

"Senator," she screamed at him, "I can see that you are no gentleman."

"I'm very sorry, Madam," the Senator replied. "But I can see that you, too, are not."

If you marry for money, you'll earn it.

♥ ☆ ♥ ☆ ♥

Humor is the lubricant, the oil that keeps the engine of marriage from getting overheated.

♥ ☆ ♥ ☆ ♥

Elsa and Chase Sanborn define the period of childhood (their kids, of course) as that period when, in order to lose weight, they bathe them.

♥ ☆ ♥ ☆ ♥

Pat Flanigan's wife had just delivered her twelfth child in a marriage of sixteen years. To celebrate, Pat's office staff gave a party for him, complete with a ceramic plate that had the Flanigan coat of arms on its surface. Pat accepted the plate with great pride, looked at it, then said, "It's great. I thank you a million. But tell me, why that odd-looking pelican on the coat of arms?"

"Pat, that's not a pelican," the office manager said. "It's a stork with his legs worn down."

Ellen Sargeant was truly worried about her husband, Bill. The poor guy had quit shaving, had not had a haircut in months, was terribly erratic about changing his clothes and she could not understand what had come over him. In desperation, she went to see the minister who told her he had noticed the dramatic change and invited her to have Bill come to see him for a conference. Within the week, Bill appeared in the minister's office. He told the minister what was bothering him. "I'm in debt up to my eyeballs. Business is just terrible. I don't know what to do."

"Let me make a suggestion," the preacher said. "Take your Bible, set it on the window sill before you retire, be sure the window is open all the way, and in the morning, wherever the wind has moved the pages, that's where you'll read and follow the advice of the Bible."

Bill followed the advice. Wonder of wonder, it worked. He was a new man, with Armani shoes, Hickey-Freeman suit, manicured hands, coifed hair and so on. The preacher invited him for a conference on this amazing change.

"Tell me, Bill, did you follow my advice?"

"You bet I did. And it worked."

"Please, then, if you don't mind...what part of the Bible was revealed to you on the wind-stirred pages, to have turned you from a loser to a winner?"

"Chapter 11!" Bill replied.

"I'll take cash and checks. - - No second mortgages."

Americans have been creating tall tales (sometimes called "whoopers", "windies", or plain old "lies" ever since we became a nation! And American tall tales made the famous Baron Munchausen, Europe's champion tall tale teller, look almost like his stuff is truth. In short, Americans are masters at the lie that we call the tall tale. It doesn't matter if we are discussing city life, country life, hunting and fishing, automobiles or airplanes, or any subject at all. We tell the best tales (lies) of any nation extant now or ever.

But it seems silly to make such statements alone. Let's prove it! Here are a few of the thousands of tales that represent the marvelous inventions of the imagination (lies!) known to man. Baron Munchausen, move over!

Charles Peters was terribly disturbed at the huge size of his winter heating bill. But, like all Illinois guys, he was a man with plenty of know-how. So he got himself put on every direct mail list he could think of and now heats his home with the tons of paper that flood his huge mailbox. And he has so derned much paper that half of it is given to this neighbors so that they can save dough by using junk mail to heat their houses too!

Optimist: A fellow who earns $100 a week, then marries...and to a woman who loves kids!

Eddie Piquant and his wife live in Edinburg, Illinois. They went to an art fair and bought a lovely winter forest scene, trees barren but beautifully symmetrical. The next spring, Eddie's wife noticed that this artful, realistic paint of maple trees showed the limbs beginning to bud. By early summer, the maples had a full set of leaves that provided real shade for the Piquants, until frost. They loved to sit under that painting, enjoying the lovely breeze and shade. Not only that, but next spring, they tapped into the trees and collected enough maple syrup to last them for a year, till next maple syrup harvest. Now you must admit that the artist was wonderfully talented, a superb realistic painter. And none appreciated him more than that artful Illinois farm family.

☆ ☆ ☆ ☆ ☆

Parental wisdom: Raising your children so that others besides yourselves, will think well of them.

Edith Somerset was the fussiest woman in all of Peoria, Illinois. They tell the story about her compulsive cleanliness. It seems that she had a cuckoo clock that chimed every hour on the hour. To be safe, Edith would put a clean cloth to catch the droppings beneath the clock just before the cuckoo emerged. Now, you must admit that Mrs. Somerset was a mighty careful housekeeper.

Love is blind, all right, but marriage is a real eye-opener.

Sam Peacock was hired by a man who had invented a tonic that was guaranteed to give the user quadrupled years more than the normal life span. Sam's wife advised him not to get involved in what seemed to her a flim-flam affair, but Sam was determined and took the job. However, he did ask to speak to satisfied customers. He demanded to know whether a particular tonic could actually quadruple the normal life span beyond three score and ten, or seventy years. "I really don't know," admitted one user. "You see, I'm only 120 years old."

Worry, stress, unease seem to be the order of the day...today. They tell the story of a businessman in Joliet, Illinois who worried so derned much about his faltering marriage that his hairpiece turned white.

Clara and Charlie Evers farm in Menard County, Illinois. Theirs is among the richest ground that can be found in Illinois. To illustrate its richness, Clara tells this story. Watermelons are a wonderful produce from their garden. One year, they grew such a big one that they decided to sell it at the Illinois State Fair. So they took this humongous melon, occupied a stall on opening day, and did real well. Here's how:
They worked a spigot into the side of the melon and sold watermelon juice for the first three days. Then they cut the melon and sold watermelon slices for the last four days of the week-long fair. Clara said that Charlie was furious because the State Fair only lasted a week and more than half of that melon was wasted.

Clara says they also raise apples. They have one tree that suffices for them and most of Menard County. Last year they picked 400 bushels off that tree and then Charlie had to go to the barn and get a ladder!

As you can well imagine, the Evers can't begin to use all the apples that tree produces. So they make cider out of some of it, usually about fifty barrels off the one tree. One year they had so much cider that they set up a roadside stand and offered it for sale. One day a city feller came along and wanted to buy some of their cider. Charlie asked how much he wanted and the customer said about thirty barrels. Charlie said he couldn't destroy an entire apple for that small an order.

Cletus Hobart says that at his house, the family eats so much rabbit meat that every time a dog barks, they all hide under the house.

Charlie and Clara also produce pork. Their herd of fifty sows keeps them busy as can be. One of the skills Charlie learned over the years was the art of hog calling. He's the best in the middle west. One time, he sucked himself full of air, let go with a tremendous hog call and hogs came asnufflin' up from Indiana, Iowa and Nebraska. There was one time when he huffed himself full of air, let out a blast of a hog call and a herd of thirty hogs came oinkin' in from California.

Charles and Clara are true conservationists...they still use windmills instead of electric power. That is, they did until the time when there wasn't enough wind, so Charlie shut down two of his three windmills and that did the job because you see, there was only enough wind for one. And when that one windmill slowed down, Charlie had to take down half his barbed wire fence to let enough wind come through to make that one lone windmill turn! Those barbed wire fences can sure block a lot of wind.

George Hatmaker is such an affable man that he lets his wife dictate all aspects of their family life. Why, that man is so hen-pecked, he molts twice a year.

Maybe Charlie and Clara were so peculiar because they had no children. Charlie once came home from a fishing trip with a lovely live bass on his line. The bass looked so pitifully at Clara that she took him off the stringer and put him in the cattle water trough. And that fish lived and did just fine. The longer they had him, the more the Evers loved him like a child. First, and by the littles, Charlie taught Stinky to waddle along beside them, taking him out of the tank a few seconds more each day, until that fish was able to take hour-long walks. Did they have fun together! Then tragedy struck. They were crossing a plank bridge and little Stinky slipped through the planks and fell into the creek where, before Charlie could get to him, he drowned! Poor fish!

One time Charlie took Clara fishing. He was an old hand at it but not Clara. So Charlie baited her hook, showed her how to cast, how to wiggle the bait and all that. Well, sure enough, Clara hooked a nice one. When she pulled it up to the boat, she looked over the side and announced, "He's a giant, Charlie. Must be at least twelve inches."

Charlie laughed like crazy, "You call that big? A twelve incher? Why, he's just newly spawned! A baby thing! Twelve inches! Haw! Haw! Haw!"

"Tiny?" Clara replied. "You call that tiny? That twelve inches is between the eyes!"

Edith Haas' sister is married to a guy so thin that you can count how many olives he has eaten!

♥ ☆ ♥ ☆ ♥

Edith, herself, is thin, absolutely shapeless. If it weren't for her elbows, kneecaps and Adam's apple, she wouldn't have a shape at all.

♥ ☆ ♥ ☆ ♥

Mrs. Edgar feeds her husband so well that he developed Dunlap's disease. You know what that is? Well, the symptoms show that his belly's dunlap-ed over his belt.

Charlie liked to fish much more than hunt, but every winter he managed to get a few days hunting done so's to have fresh rabbit and quail on the table. And he had a wonderful hunting dog named Ginger. And was she smart! Why, when he carried his gun on his left shoulder, the dog pointed quail. When the gun was on his right shoulder, Ginger pointed rabbit. And when the gun was in hand at arm's length, that dog went to pointing ducks.

Well, one day, Charlie got out the brand new fishing pole Clara had given him and, in few minutes, Ginger came out from the timber, holding twixt her teeth, a big can of worms.

The Evers family comprised several generations of farmers, all on the same farm. They were very proud of their historic, centuries-old history record, near Middletown. When Charlie's father retired from the farm, he moved to Middletown and lived twenty more years. Every day, he'd go to the courthouse and sit on the steps, enjoying the sunlight. Never missed a day. And do you know that for a solid week after the old man died, his shadow still showed up on the courthouse steps!

Their neighbors are weird, too. One neighbor woman was viciously gored by a bull as she was walking across the cow pasture. Her husband ran to her rescue and, seeing the problem, quickly ran to the sheep shed, killed a ewe, removed the innards and placed them carefully inside his wife's belly, to replace those the bull had hooked out. Well, the woman recovered just fine and do you know that every year, they shear at least thirty pounds of wool off her! And she's now an easy keeper, as they say. Why? Because she eats only grass-like stuff such as lettuce, spinach, bean pods and cornstalks.

♥ ☆ ♥ ☆ ♥

But, with it all, Charlie and Clara lived a happy life. Still, it was real sad the way Clara passed away. It seems that she and Charlie were shingling the barn and Charlie made her wear rubber boots to keep her from slipping and falling off the roof. Well, she never slipped but she did stumble and then skidded off the roof. But it was wonderful because she landed on the ground on her feet. But it was not so wonderful when she began to bounce because of those rubber boots. Up and down she went, never stopping. Day and night, up and down, until Charlie had to shoot her to keep her from starving to death.

In Dayton, Ohio, they tell about a wife whose cooking was so bad that the flies held a conference and decided to repair the screens on the windows.

4
GOLF

Golf is often the source of great family joy and -- not so often -- family aggravation. Here are a few situations where husbands and wives used -- or were considering using -- their golf clubs in ways manufacturers hadn't considered when they produced them.

"Sweetheart, today is our wedding anniversary. Do you remember that great day in our lives?"

"Boy, do I! Why, that was the day I sank a twenty-five foot putt!"

"Here I've gone and fixed an elaborate lunch but you haven't noticed. All you think about is golf, golf, golf."

"That's not true, honey. Now if you'd please pass the putter..."

"Your husband is sure playing better now that he's got a new stance."

"Old stance...new husband."

A girl dressed in her wedding gown came running down the fairway toward the eighth hole. She was waving her arms and screaming, "George, what do you mean by this. We've all been at the church for hours, waiting for you!"

"Susie," he said, shaking his head, "if I've told you once, I've told you twenty times...only if it rains, only if it rains!"

"Hey, Doctor, we've got an emergency! The baby just swallowed all my tees."

"I'll be there at once."

"But tell me what to do till you get here, Doctor."

"Practice your putting."

"YOU GAVE ME A CHOICE, AND I MADE IT!"

"Oh, Daddy, I had to call you. George has gone and left me."
"Don't worry, Dear. You know and I know that he's run out on you twice before."
"Yeah, I know, but this time, he took his golf clubs."

"How'd the game go today, Dear? Did you win?"
"No, but I got a lot of practice. I got to hit the ball more than anyone else."

A golfing parson, badly beaten by an elderly parishioner, returned to the club house depressed.
"Cheer up," said his opponent. "Remember, you win eventually. You'll be burying me someday."
"Yes," said the parson. "But even then, it'll be your hole."

"Paul, you promised to come home by six. Here it is seven o'clock and you're just coming in off the course. What happened?"

"Oh, shucks, we just got delayed all afternoon. First Tommy had to fix a flat tire. Then we ran into a long line at the first tee. Then we had to pause and wait for a thunderstorm to end. Then Eldon dropped dead on the tenth green."

"What! Eldon dropped...dead? How terrible."

"And that wasn't the worst of it. From then on, there was nothing to do but hit the ball, then drag Eldon, hit the ball and drag Eldon...all afternoon. Now do you understand why I was so late?"

Did you hear about the Mexican-American couple, Marie and Juan, both avid golfers. In fact, the only time they were able to get along amicably was on the golf course. But finally things reached an impasse and Marie shot a hole in Juan.

Technology has really come to the golf course. Witness the incident where Elmer and Rose, husband and wife, were playing in different foursomes on the same course. Elmer took his phone and called his wife: "Hey, Selma. Just trying out the new phone I've got with me. What hole you on?"

"The 14th. But hold just a minute, Elmer, my **other** phone is ringing."

Eddie Foy's wife was new at the game. On one hole, she swung and managed to cut loose a huge divot of turf. "What do I do with this chunk of soil, Dear?" she asked.

"I'd suggest that we take it home and use it to start a garden."

The husband and wife foursome had played together for many years. But one day, Emily Scroggins noticed that their friends and opponents were having trouble. She took husband Bill's arm and said, "Bill, I think Paul is having a stroke!"

Bill looked carefully at Paul. "Well, I feel sure he'll put it on his card."

A local preacher, not too experienced at golf, asked the local pro to play a round with him. The pro was unbearable in his fun-making of the preacher and kidded him unmercifully. When they got back to the clubhouse, the preacher said, "I invite you to play with me again next week. And do bring your parents for a foursome. After the game, maybe I'll marry them!"

"It's golf, golf, golf, morning, noon and night. Why don't you take up some other sport, like polo!" his wife complained.

"That's not much different than golf, dear. In fact it IS golf...with fertilizer."

"My husband is a golf nut," Helen complained. "But it does have one advantage...it makes him take showers."

Percy Boyer claims his wife approves of his taking up the sport of golf. "In fact," Percy says, "she'd be in favor of any sport that provokes an argument."

It was a perfect day for golf, sunny, cloudless, a lovely blue sky. The Judge was hearing a divorce trial but could not keep his mind in the courtroom. The golf course kept interfering with the lawsuit! He tuned in, once again, on the case before him, hearing: "More than that, Your Honor, my client claims that the defendant, her husband, beat her senseless with a golf club."

"How many strokes?" the Judge asked absently.

Eddie and Paul were teeing off but Eddie was taking a very long time, adjusting his posture, his stance. "What's wrong, Eddie? Something bothering you?" Paul asked.

"Well, my wife came with me today and she's watching us from the club house, over there. I want to make sure this is an A-number-one shot."

"Holy Smokes, Eddie. You haven't a ghost of a chance of hitting her from here."

George Peters was depressed and his wife asked why. "Well, all the guys at the club are afraid to play with me and so my handicap is terribly high. What do you think my handicap is, Dear? You'll be amazed."

"My guess would be it's your breath."

Amos and Ruth played golf together every Sunday. So, on this particular Sunday, Amos's birthday, they celebrated with a lunch, consisting of, mainly, whiskey. Thoroughly liquified, they went to the course, played five holes, whereupon Amos asked, "The score, Ruth, how do we stand?"

"Derned if I know, Amos. But I'd say it was a miracle."

A physician's wife, left alone every Sunday, protested to her husband: "Elmer, how is it that you never ask me to play golf with you?"

"My Dear," the hubby replied, "there are just three events in a person's life that must be done alone: testify, die and putt!"

"JUST HOW EARLY ARE YOU TEEING OFF?"

Mary Owens loved the game but was not very good at it. She was out on the links one day, playing with her husband, Todd. As usual, every time she swung at the ball, she made the earth beneath it fly every which way! "My goodness, Todd," she said, blushing at her ineptitude, "I bet the worms think there's an earthquake going on."

"Don't be so sure, Mary. The worms on this course are mighty smart. My guess is that most of them are hiding beneath your golf ball for safety."

Mark Twain accompanied a lady friend to the golf course and watched while she played. But the lady moved more dirt than golf balls and, pretty soon, Mark Twain was covered with the dust she raised trying to hit the ball. Then, about half way through the course, the lady asked, "Mr. Twain, how do you like this course?"

"It's the best I ever tasted," Mark responded.

That game may have prompted him to remark: "Golf is a good walk spoiled."

Harry and Reba Silver were up in years, but still played golf, their favorite game. Naturally, they were deliberate, even slow at moving along from hole to hole. An impatient man behind them kept needling them to move faster, ever faster until Harry grew sick and tired of his remarks. "Listen, young man," he growled at the impatient fellow behind them. "I was a golfer, playing regularly before you were born."

"OK, OK," the younger fellow said, "but I'd sure appreciate it if you'd try to finish before I die."

"Charlie, how come you're using two caddies, today?"
"Cause my wife tells me that I don't spend enough time with my kids."

"How's your golf game these days, Mary?"
"Pretty good. I'm shooting in the low seventies."
"Honestly?"
"What the heck has that got to do with it?"

"Caddy, tell me...how much are 3 and 5 and 4?"
"Eight."
"Fine. You're the caddy for me."

"Al, dear, when do I get to use my putter?" his wife asked.
"Anytime before dark, Dear."

"How many strokes on this course so far, Honey?"
"Three," his wife replied.
"Three! But I counted four..."
"That was only a practice swing."
"But, Dear, tell me...why then did you cuss?"

Did you hear about the novice golfer who was so dumb that he searched a solid week for diamonds in the rough?

A wife who had never before played golf, was standing ready to tee-off on her very first drive ever. "How do you begin the game, Dear?" she asked.

"If you'll look straight ahead, you'll see a flag. Try to put the ball as close as possible to it."

His wife hit an incredible drive and hubby couldn't believe what he saw...the ball lay only inches from the cup.

"Now, what do I do?" his wife asked.

"You putt the ball into the cup, Dear."

"**NOW** you tell me!"

"How come you don't play golf with Paul Brown?" his wife asked.

"Let me ask you...would you play golf with a man who talks while you're trying to putt, changes his score and kicks his ball out of the rough when you're not looking?"

"I should say not!"

"Neither would Paul Brown."

◆ ◆ ◆ ◆ ◆

If you can smile and laugh when all around you have gone nuts, well, you must be the caddy.

"OH, ALL RIGHT THEN. GO PLAY GOLF."

Recently married, the new young wife was trying to understand the game that occupied so much of her husband's time.

"Tell me, Dear, what is a handicapped golfer?"

"He's the guy who plays with his boss."

Eddie Bogan was known as the cheapest, most penny-pinching member of the club. Why, the man had been using the same golf ball for twenty-five years. Then, one day, he walked into the club shop to buy another ball and said, "Howdy, folks, here I am again."

"George, we've been waiting for you for an hour! Why so late?"

"Well, it's Sunday, and I had to toss a coin to see whether church or golf."

"But why so dadblamed late?"

"Well, I had to toss at least fifteen times."

Have you heard that there was recently published, a dictionary of golfing terms but it was a total flop? They banned it from the mails.

Two ladies were discussing the one girl's husband. "Ben has gotten too fat for the game," she said. The other remarked, "I agree with you. Why, when he puts the ball where he can see it, he can't hit it. And when he puts the ball where he can hit it, he can't see it."

A twosome was moving down the Charleston Valley Golf Club fairway and one of the two was heard to say: "Take it easy, George. No! Now! Now! Don't let yourself get angry. Easy does it, George. Just...take...it...easy, George."

One of the caddies remarked, "I sure admire how you support and help your partner with those thoughtful words, Sir."

"My partner? He's Pete. I'm George."

"COME ON, WE'RE LATE! . . . WHAT TOOK YOU SO LONG?"

"Reverend Thornapple, I must tell you that I truly admire the way you refrain from cussing, swearing on the golf course."

"Thank you for the kind words," the pastor replied. "But I must tell you that where I spit, the grass never grows there again."

"You're the smart-aleckiest caddy I ever had!" the golfer shouted at her caddy. "And when I get back, I'm going to report you to the caddy master."

"By that time, I'll certainly be too old anyway, Ma'am."

A priest was set to drive his ball out of the sand trap and what did he do but hit into another trap just like the first. Quietly, he pursed his lips and said nothing. His fellow priest, his partner, remarked: "That's the most profane silence I have ever heard."

"Because I've caddied for you for so many years, Mr. Beavers, I feel that I have the right to tell you your game, today, is awfully inconsistent."

"Well, you see, Caddie, I'm just getting accustomed for tomorrow, for Husband-and-Wife Day."

The first female Attorney General of the United States was also an avid golfer. When she and her husband played golf, they delegated the customary secret service men to protect the twosome. There was only one problem...they had to pay the agents combat pay!

Mary Swanson was a first-rate golfer but her husband was a dud! One day, he asked her, "Mary, please tell me, what's wrong with my game?"

"I can do that," she replied. "You lift your elbow, raise it far too much...especially on the 19th hole."

George and Henrietta had played golf once a week during their entire marriage. One day, George hovered over a putt for far too long and Henrietta impatiently said, "What are you doing for goodness sake, praying?"

"I finished that long ago, Henrietta. Now I'm waiting for an answer."

"Hey, Jones, why don't you help your wife find her ball so we can play through?"

"She's found her ball. Now she's looking for her club."

Henry Palmer was teaching his wife how to play golf. "Now look at the cup, dear. Do you see the two balls at the cup? Yes? Well, if you saw four, that'd mean you had too much to drink. Understand?"

"But, dear...there's only one ball there."

Peter and Nancy Drew were dairy farmers right next door to the municipal golf course. One day, they were called to the door to confront a golfer who had just sliced a ball into their pasture, killing a fine milk cow. "I'm awfully embarrassed, Sir," the golfer said. "I hate it that I killed your fine cow. Can I replace her?"

Peter looked at Nancy, then leaned over and whispered in her ear and nodded. "That'd be OK with us. But first we want to know how many gallons a day **you** give?"

Sandy Peron was an expert golfer while her husband was anything but. One day, he asked, "Have you any suggestions as to how I can improve my game, dear?"

"You might try laying off for, say, thirty days."

"And after that?"

"Just quit."

"Mrs. Golden, has the club tournament committee approved your husband's qualifying game?"

"Don't think so. But they did ask for fiction rights."

chon
Day

Wife:	"How'd you do at the new club?"
Husband:	"Not bad at all. I shot a 69."
Wife:	"Wow! That was might good, for you. You gonna play tomorrow?"
Husband:	"Sure am. Tomorrow, I'm going after the second hole."

Martha and Ben Barnes applied for membership in an exclusive Miami Beach golf club and were refused. A kindly member saw how dejected they were and suggested the name of another club.

A friend told the chagrined couple, "they probably thought you were Jewish."

At the second club, Martha and Ben were accepted. He announced at once, "Please tell all members that Martha and I are not Jewish."

"What! But everybody in this club is Jewish," was the reply.

"Well, I'm a sonovabitch," Ben exclaimed.

"If you'd only mentioned that earlier, you'd never have been rejected at the other club."

A golf links has been defined as the best place for a girl to find a husband.

Fred Hoffman says his wife goes round the course in less and less every month, but, unfortunately, her game hasn't improved.

Those who don't golf can't appreciate the hold that sport has on those who love it. Consider the case of Norm Susart, whose wife had just given him an ultimatum! "Either you quit leaving me to go on golf outings every weekend or I'm going to move out, go home to mother and stay there!"

Norm's response? "Gosh, I'm sure going to miss you."

"Are you sure it's not out of your way?"

"Martha! What's this I hear about our having a son?"

"WELL, I'VE TRIMMED OUR BUDGET DOWN TO BARE ESSENTIALS—FOOD, CLOTHING AND GREEN FEES."

5

EPITAPH

It seems quite appropriate to have this final chapter of husband and wife humor devoted entirely to a kind of "grave" humor. Not to *dig* too deeply into the problem or throw *stones* at the solution or play up the *turf* involved, we yet offer a peek at what some husbands and wives have considered appropriate as they put aside the experiences of a lifetime and lay to rest the joys and sorrows of their marriage.

*****

Hatfield, Mass.
Beneath this stone
        A lump of clay
Lies Arabella Young
Who on the 21st of May
        1771
Began to hold her tongue.

*****

Sargentville, Maine
Sacred to the memory of
Elisha Philbrook and his wife Sarah

Beneath these stones do lie,
Back to back, my wife and I!
When the last trumpet the air shall fill
If she gets up, I'll lie still.

*****

My life is done, my Race is run
My resting place is here.
This stone is got to keep the Spot
Lest men should dig too near.
        Manchester, Connecticut. 1790.

*****

A rum cough carried him off.
        Stowe, Vermont

This stone was erected by the deceased's brother, certainly not his wife!

Knight's Corner,
Pelham, Mass

Warren Gibbs
Died by arsenic poison
March 23, 1860 Age 36 years
5 months and 23 days

Think my friends when this you see
How my wife has dealt with me
She in some oysters did prepare
Some poison for my lot and share
Then of the same I did partake
And nature yielded to its fate
Before she my wife became
Mary Felton was her name.

Erected by his Brother
Wm. Gibbs

* * * * *

Here lies the body of Obadiah Wilkinson
And Ruth, his wife
Their warfare is accomplished.
New Haven, Connecticut

* * * * *

Death is a Debt
To Nature Due
Which I have Paid
And so must you.

* * * * *

Mr. John Pannel killed by a tree
in seventeen hundred & seventy three.

* * * * *

Epitaph on the grave of a hypochondriac:
"I told you I was sick!"

He came to take life's bitter cup
Then turned his aching head aside
Disgusted with the taste, he died.
Bar Harbor, Maine - 1749

* * * * *

Under the sod
Under the trees
Lies the body of Jonathan Pease.
He is not here
But only his pod
He has shelled his peas
And gone to God.

* * * *

Dentist's epitaph in a Connecticut cemetery:
"When on this tomb you gaze with gravity,
Cheer up! I'm filling my LAST CAVITY."

* * * * *

Here lies one Wood enclosed in wood,
One wood within another
The outer wood is very good,
We cannot praise the other.
Winslow, Maine

* * * * *

Here are some wonderfully funny old epitaphs found on tombstones in New England. Sometimes they tell the story of a life, other times they tell the story of what the husband, wife, family thought about the dead soul. One thing is sure, Americans from the first have never abandoned their sense of humor, even in death. These are from *"Quaint Epitaphs,"* Susan Darling Safford, published in 1898.

* * * * *

We can but mourn our loss,
Though wretched was his life.
Death took him from the cross,
Erected by his wife.

Charity wife of Gideon Bligh
Underneath this stone doth lie.
Naught was she e'er known to do
That which her husband told her to.

＊ ＊ ＊ ＊ ＊

Here lies the wife of brother Thomas,
Whom tyrant death has torn from us,
Her husband never shed a tear,
Until his wife was buried here.
And then he made a fearful rout,
For fear she might find her way out.

＊ ＊ ＊ ＊ ＊

Peggy Dow shared the vicissitudes of Lorenzo Dow fifteen years,
and died aged 39.

＊ ＊ ＊ ＊ ＊

TABITHA, wife of MOSES FLEDGER
Aged 55
(Job printing neatly done)

＊ ＊ ＊ ＊ ＊

He got a fish bone in his throat
And then he sang an angel's note.

＊ ＊ ＊ ＊ ＊

This corpse
is
Phoebe Thorps

＊ ＊ ＊ ＊ ＊

He's done a-catching cod.
And gone to meet his God.

＊ ＊ ＊ ＊ ＊

Here lies my wife in earthly mould,
Who when she lived did naught but scold.
Peace! Wake her not, for now she's still,
She had, but now I have my will.

Some have children, others none,
Here lies the mother of twenty-one.

*****

A man had cremated four wives and the ashes, kept in four urns, being overturned and fallen together, were buried together, at last, with this inscription:
Stranger pause and shed a tear,
For Mary Jane lies buried here.
Mingled in a most surprising manner
With Susan, Marie and portions of Hannah.

*****

Sacred to the remains of Jonathan Thompson, a pious Christian and affectionate husband.
His disconsolate widow still continues to carry on his business at the old place since her bereavement.

*****

Here lies the body of Mary Ford
We hope her soul is with the Lord.
But if for Tophet, she's changed this life,
Better be there than J. Ford's wife.

*****

Here lies Jane Smith,
Wife of Thomas Smith, Marble Cutter.
This monument was erected by her husband as a tribute to her memory and a specimen of his work.
Monuments of the same style are two hundred and fifty dollars.

*****

The winter snow congealed his form
But now we know our Uncle's warm.

*****

Our papa dear has gone to Heaven
To make arrangements for eleven.

Here lies my wife, a sad slatterned shrew
If I said I regretted her, I should lie too.

*****

Her lies Ann Mann.
She lived an old maid
But died an old Mann.

*****

Listen, Mother, Aunt and me
Were killed, here we be.
We should not had time to missle
Had they blown the engine whistle.

*****

Plainfield, Vermont 1888
Five times five years, I lived a virgin's life
Nine times five years, I lived a virtuous wife;
Wearied of this mortal life, I rest.

*****

There was a nice fellow from Fife,
Who had a blow-up with his wife.
He lost half his toes
Two thirds of his nose,
An ear, four teeth and his life.

*****

(It pays to advertise, even in a graveyard!)

Lincoln, Maine
Sacred to the Memory
of
Jared Bates
who died Aug. the 6th, 1800

His widow, aged 24, lives at
7 Elm Street, has every
qualification for a good wife,
and years to be comforted.

One hesitates here because of the possibility of the wrong impression. Still, subtlety does have a place in final situations.

Hollis, N.H.

Cynthia Stevens
Here lies Cynthia, Steven's wife
She lived six years in calms and strife.
Death came at least and set her free,
I was glad and so was she.

* * * * *

It certainly paid to die back then... "twelve dollar coffin"? Undertakers, please note.

Burlington, Mass.

Anthony Drake
Sacred to the memory of Anthony Drake
Who died for peace and quietness sake;
His wife was constantly scolding and scoffin,
So he thought repose in a twelve dollar coffin.

* * * * *

But how could they be sure?

Canaan, N. H.

Amos Shute
1789-1842
He heard the angels calling him
From the Celestial Shore
He flapped his wings and away he went
To make one angel more.

* * * * *

Stop here, my friend, and cast an eye,
As you are now, so once was I,
As I am now, so you must be
So prepare for death and follow me.

(Someone wrote under the above epitaph, the following.)

To follow you I'm not content
Unless I know which way you went.

For some husbands it seems as though it is never too late to admit a mistake.

Little Compton, R.I.

Two upright stones of the same size; on one:

In memory of Lidia ye wife of Mr. Simeon
Palmer who died Dec. ye 26th, 1754 in ye 35th year
of her age.

On the other:

In memory of Elizabeth, who should have been
the wife of Mr. Simeon Palmer, who died August 14th
1776 in the 64th year of her age.

✳ ✳ ✳ ✳ ✳

It seems most appropriate to add, "May she rest in peace, having lived a very long and busy life." Not even the Bible lists anyone as productive as she.

Litchfield, Conn.

Here lies the body of Mrs. Mary, wife of
Deacon John Buel, Esq. She died Nov. 4, 1768,
aged 90--having had 13 children, 101 Grand-
children, 247 Grate-Grand children, and 49
Grate-Grate-Grand children; total 410.
Three Hundred and Thirty Six Survived Her.

✳ ✳ ✳ ✳ ✳

At age 37, poor Shute deserved a rhyme this cute.

Canaan, N.H.

Sarah Shute
1803-1840

Here lies, cut down like unripe fruit,
The wife of Deacon Amos Shute;
She died of drinking too much coffee,
Anno Dominy, Eighteen forty.

We had never heard of Boulder, Illinois. Neither do we want to, ever again. On the other hand, maybe our international peace-talkers could get a good lesson from those talkers of Boulder, Illinois.

Boulder, Ill.

Alice Phillips
First and last wife of Thomas Phillips
Talked to death by friends.

* * * * *

One can only assume that Dr. Rothwell was a mighty successful free-loader.

Oak Grove Cemetery
Pawtucket, R. I.

Rothwell
William P. Rothwell, M.D.
1866-1939

This is on me.
R.

* * * * *

An entirely appropriate dedication to a jeweler who obviously also repaired watches:

Bennett's Cemetery,
Canisteo, N. Y.

Thial Clark

In memory of
Thial Clark, the Jeweler, who has quit running but is wound up in hopes of being taken in hand by the Supreme Master machinist for repairs and to be adjusted and set running for the world to come again.

So mote it be.

Some guys just can't make it here. Let's hope he did/does better at his next stop.

Riverside Cemetery
Asheville, N.C.

Campbell
"Meant well, tried a little, failed much."

* * * * *

It certainly pays to read the instructions on the bottle!

Burlington, Mass.

Susan Lowder
Here lies the body of Susan Lowder
Who burst while drinking Seidlitz powder;
Called from this world to her heavenly rest
She should have waited till it effervesced.

* * * * *

It pays to "watch your language!"

Cripple Creek, Col.

He called
Bill Smith
A Liar

* * * * *

It also pays to be quicker on the draw.

Princess Anne Co., Va.

Here lies the body of Henry Moore
Who got in the way of a 44.

* * * * *

They say that this old boy was an atheist. One might have guessed that from his telling inscription.

Vancouver, Washington

Haine
haint

A very practical, useful inscription, given the obvious condition of the deceased.

Lee, Mass.

Mrs. Alpha White, weighed 309 pounds
Open wide ye golden gates
That lead to the heavenly shore.
Our father suffered in passing through
And mother weighed much more.

✳ ✳ ✳ ✳ ✳

Perhaps this telling inscription was the precursor, the beginning, of our truth-in-advertising regulations.

Girard, Pa.

Ellen Shannon
Aged 26 years
Who was Fatally Burned
March 21st 1870
By the explosion of a lamp
filled with "R. E. Danforth's
Non-Explosive Burning Fluid."

✳ ✳ ✳ ✳ ✳

Eat not too much nor too fast...if you would last.

Savannah, Ga.

Here lies old Rastus Sominy
Died a-eating hominy
In 1859 anno domini.

✳ ✳ ✳ ✳ ✳

Maybe he/she was modest or, perhaps, the "mind-your-own business," type of person, in death as in life.

Stowe, Vt.

I was Somebody -- who, is no
Business of Yours

225

Synonyms, synonyms, always we evade using the term "death." Or perhaps they liked the way "inanimate" rhymed with "68"?

Highland Cemetery, Dover, N.H.

Joseph & Betsy Hartwell

Repository
of
Joseph Hartwell, Inanimate
April 7, 1867, Aet. 68
Betsy Hartwell, Inanimate
Dec. 7, 1862, Aet. 68

✳ ✳ ✳ ✳ ✳

One must conclude that Ivy Saunders was a might poor judge of husband material.

Shutesbury, Mass.

To the Four Husbands
Of Miss Ivy Saunders
1790, 1794, 1808, 18??

Here lies my husbands, One, Two, Three
Dumb as men could ever be;
As for my Fourth, well, praise be God
He bides for a little above the sod;
Alex, Ben, Sandy were the first three's names
And to make things tidy I'll add his -- James.

✳ ✳ ✳ ✳ ✳

Political affiliations dominate the lives of many, even up to the point (and beyond?) of death.

Bethel Cemetery, St. Louis, Mo.

B. H. Morris
Died April, 1900

"Kind friends
I leave behind
Cast your votes
For Wm. J. Bryan"

Baton Rouge, La.

Here lies the body of David Jones.
His last words were: "I die a Christian
and a Democrat."

* * * * *

It's wonderful to see humor deliberately employed on a gravestone. Everyone has heard of "bigmouthed" people. But old Mulvaney "takes the cake!"

Middleford, Mass.

Thomas Mulvaney
1724-1795
Old Thomas Mulvaney lies here
His mouth ran from ear to ear
Reader, tread lightly on this wonder
For if he yawns you're gone by thunder.

* * * * *

As winter draws to a close, we hear it said everywhere, "I can't wait till Spring!" Well, Uncle Peter didn't.

Medway, Mass.

In memory of Mr.
Peter Daniels
Born Aug 7, 1688
Dyed May 30, 1746

Beneath this stone,
    A lump of clay,
Lies Uncle Peter Daniels
Who too early
    In the month of May
Took off his winter flannels.

* * * * *